2

ISSN 2152-9000 (print)
ISSN 2152-9027 (online)
ISBN 978-0-9831580-0-4

No. 2 ◆ Tools
Copyright © 2010 by The Pedestrian Quarterly, LLC

The Pedestrian is published quarterly by
    The Pedestrian Quarterly, LLC
    PO Box 22468
    Philadelphia, PA 19110
    USA

Subscription rates for 1 year (4 issues) in US dollars:
    United States: $32
    Canada: $44
    Elsewhere: $55

For uninterrupted service, send address changes to the mailing address above, use the subscriber's online account, or email info@thepedestrian.org.

To distribute The Pedestrian, contact info@thepedestrian.org.

Edited by Christopher Spiker

The Pedestrian

2

TOOLS

Contents

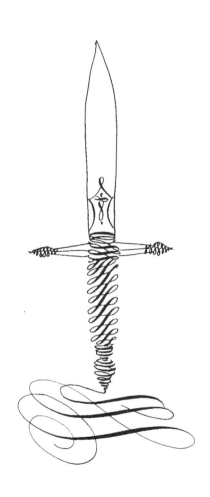

Introduction

AFTER SEVERAL DAYS in which I brainstormed potential topics for this issue, a lecture on Robert Frost and his well-known poem "Mowing" prompted me to consider *tools*. But could I collect enough good essays on the topic to fill an entire issue? I thought of Scott Russell Sanders' much anthologized essay, "The Inheritance of Tools", which reminded me that one's tools often evoke vivid memories – a promising start. Then I thought of Hilaire Belloc's "The Mowing of a Field", which perfectly captures the wonderful monotony of an expertly wielded tool:

> Then, again, get yourself into a mechanical and repetitive mood: be thinking of anything at all but your mowing, and be anxious only when there seems some interruption to the monotony of the sound. In this mowing should be like one's prayers – all of a sort and always the same, and so made that you can establish a monotony and work them, as it were, with half your mind: that happier half, the half that does not bother.

There is indeed something happy and carefree about that "mechanical and repetitive mood", whether one is mowing a lawn; securing floor boards with hammer and nails; striking sharp-angled, cross-court forehands with a trusty tennis racket; crocheting a hat; or peeling an apple. When we become accomplished in any of these activities our use of the tool slips into our subconscious. The tool becomes a part of us.

Perhaps this explains our frequent attachment to one or another tool and the memories that we associate with it. I, for example, hadn't given any thought for nearly two decades to a man-powered rotary edger that my parents owned. But as I thought through the various tools that I have used, I was struck by my vivid memories of using that rusty, squeaky, rough-handled edger to cut the grass that had grown over our sidewalks. I was surprised by how clearly I remembered the way the brown paint of the handle would rub off on my hands; the rhythm of the sudden *jerk*-forward-stop, *jerk*-forward-stop motion; and the occasional, abrupt halt of one of the spokes against a rock, which would throw the handle's butt into my rib cage and violently knock the wind out of me. I would set out with the lofty ambition of sculpting our lawn into an artform but was always disappointed. The lawn was elevated (or the sidewalk sunken), and the final sight was that of a slightly snakelike line of grass sitting atop an ugly inch or two of mud next to the sidewalk. But if the result was often disappointing, the actual use of the edger was indeed happy and carefree, providing time to think of other things – wiffleball stats, a tennis tournament, the future value of a stamp collection, or, best yet, nothing at all.

I enjoyed reading and considering many essays related to this topic, my favorites of which are shared here. I will let the essays speak for themselves. Thanks to everyone who contributed. ❧

[THE EDITOR]

CHRIS ARTHUR

An Essay on the Esse*

I

*T*HE ESSE WAS the heart of the house. To cast it thus is neither accurate – beyond a few rough similarities – nor original, but it's the best way I can think of to convey the role it played. The Esse's heat circulated invisibly, providing a background warmth in all the rooms, making them seem welcoming and lived in. It kept the water at the right temperature for baths, the gentle gurgling in the pipes that ran between it and the tank was companionable, like a softly spoken conversation between friends. When my mother became too frail to stoke it and the Esse was finally removed, it was almost as if the house had died. The whole place felt different. The rooms became icy and uninviting; the rumbling bass voice of the pipes fell silent, replaced by the periodic robotic whir of an electric immersion heater. Without the Esse an unlived in mustiness took hold. Putting in less labor-intensive devices for cooking and water heating was like major surgery that hadn't worked.

---

*   From *Irish Elegies* (Palgrave Macmillan, 2009).

The patient survived, but only as a shadow of who they'd been before. Arteries were left irreparably damaged, allowing the precious hemoglobin of the Esse's embers to seep away. As a result, despite the new prostheses, the place was starved of the oxygen of warmth on which it so depended. Soon an atmosphere of sepulchral airlessness descended and the house no longer felt like home.

The essay is at the heart of my life. To cast it thus may seem to put a perilous reliance upon words, but it conveys how much I value this peculiar genre. Of course I would survive without it — it is *at* the heart, not the heart itself — but its absence now would seem as serious a loss as the Esse's removal from the house. Essays provide the frames within which I can draw my pictures of the world. They offer parsing lenses which help me bring the grammar of experience into focus. Making these little fires of prose provides the psyche with the warmth of meaning that it craves. I know they're small-scale, tentative, unable to cast more than a flickering of heat and light. Essays don't possess the incandescence of those great pyres and furnaces lit by science, art, religion (though they do steal many sparks from them); they're more like campfires than conflagrations. Essays allow for individual articulation. They can be molded into any shape. The sticks they offer me to rub together allow the kindling of flames that fit the hearth of my particular being, where other fires might scorch it or just gutter and go out. Essays let me trace with words the contours of the mind's invisible topography, without imposing the iron of disfiguring insistence. They eschew those molten certainties that cool into the deadweight of dogma. Conversational not analytic, essays are more akin to the Esse's rumbling voice in the water pipes than the immersion heater's bursts of clipped impersonal diction. Where the Esse's squat iron presence exerted a kind of gravity, pulling domestic life into its daily rhythms, the gravitational pull of essays invites thoughts, memories, and reflections into new orbits, allowing them to crystallize into unexpected forms.

II

THE ESSE WAS the focal point in the kitchen at Whiteways, our family home near Belfast. The name referred to the white roughcast walls that set the house apart from the red brick of all the neighboring dwellings. The Esse occupied a made-to-measure tiled niche. Because of the kitchen's small size, the niche wasn't large enough for an Aga, my mother's originally preferred make of stove – the type her mother had used and which her two sisters likewise favored. Once the Esse was installed, though, she had the convert's enthusiasm and soon sang its praises over any Aga. The niche's pale yellow tiles matched the color of the Esse's front and sides. Its top was black, with a shiny silver bolster in the middle of the hob. Raising the bolster revealed the hotplate on which the kettle was boiled and saucepans were heated. On either side of the bolster were heavy circular metal lids, set flush with the stove's surface. These could be lifted by hooking a special metal implement into indentations shaped to take it. It was like fitting a giant key into a hot, heavy plug and pulling it out. The left hand lid gave access to the burning embers held safely in the Esse's core. It was opened twice a day to feed the fire with anthracite. The right hand lid led to a shallow empty chamber whose function I never discovered. At the front was a fire door and two heavy oven doors, thickly insulated to keep in the heat. The doors swung back on special hinges and their noise on opening and closing was an important theme in the signature tune of familiarity played out every day by the ensemble of object-instruments about the house. Their accustomed sounds were only noticed if some variation intruded, changing a repertoire recognized since infancy. It lulled me into that sense of belonging which the noises in all our encampments and habitations variously provide.

The Esse's fire door was opened to rake the grate. This was done using the same metal implement that lifted the fuel hatch. In fact we called it "the rake", though it bore no similarity to the garden variety. It was more like a thick metal ruler, hooked at one end, narrowed to its key shape at the other. The keyed end used to lift the fuel hatch also fitted a slot in the grate. If you then pulled vigorously backward and forward the live coals were jostled, showering their ash into the ash-pan below and making room for fresh anthracite to keep the fire alight. The ash-pan was emptied first thing in the morning and last thing at night – pulling it out with the hooked end of the rake and using this as a handle to carry the burning load to the metal bin outside the kitchen door. A hod for fuel stood beside the bin. This was filled by using it like a giant scoop on the pile of anthracite kept in a nearby outhouse. Upending the hod, its blunt snout fitted into the Esse's open fuel hatch, sent a load of anthracite sliding noisily into the stove's dark innards. These days I rarely smell hot anthracite ash, but if I do it transports me to a vanished world as surely as any madeleine.

The essay became a focal point in my life seemingly by accident. In 1989, I bought a copy of that year's *Best American Essays*, the annual collection that scours the literary magazines, harvesting a yearly crop of excellence. At that point I'd never heard of the series – then only in its fourth year – or of the series' editor, Robert Atwan, who has done so much to assist in what he describes as the genre's "remarkable literary comeback". My knowledge of essays then was very slight. I'm not sure why I bought *Best American Essays 1989*. Its dowdy grey cover didn't make it the sort of volume likely to stand out – although it's possible, I suppose, that the brash cacophony of covers that's become so commonplace in bookshops now meant the sated eye found its dullness interesting. Or maybe what appealed was the promise of Atwan's opening words, that the gathered essays "are intimate, candid, revealing, close to the pulse of human experience". For whatever reason, my browsing that day in an Edinburgh bookshop led me to a book that was to have a profound impact on my life. I read it avidly, almost at a sitting, then started to write essays and read about the form. It was as if discovering this clutch of brilliant exemplars acted to legitimate and release a reservoir of words that had been building up for years in some hidden nest inside. My first essay, "Ferrule", seemed to emerge pre-formed, as if already laid. I had a crucial stroke of beginner's luck with it – "Ferrule" was accepted for publication by the first journal to which I offered it, *The American Scholar*, then under the editorship of Joseph Epstein, one of the essayists included in *Best American Essays 1989*, and someone whose books of essays I subsequently went on to read and learn from. I published essays in a range of other journals and then in book form – *Irish Nocturnes*, *Irish Willow*, *Irish Haiku*, and now *Irish Elegies*. I've not stopped writing essays, or reading about them, since that defining moment in 1989 when I first encountered Atwan's series.

Thinking about essays now, I remember the niche into which the Esse at Whiteways so snugly fitted. The essay seemed tailor-made to fill a niche that was waiting in my psyche. I'd tried my hand at poetry, fiction, academic prose, but despite some modest successes it had always felt as if I was cooking on stoves that didn't fit my kitchen. It wasn't until the essay fell into my lap, courtesy of that *Best*

American Essays volume, that I found a genre in which I felt at home. The freedom and flexibility of essays appealed, as did their tradition of independent individuality, their scant regard for authority, their love of language. It's a hard form to define – in fact I'd agree with G. Douglas Atkins that essays represent "an implicit critique of the drive towards definition" – and yet some characterizations do catch something of their elusive spirit. For example, Edward Hoagland suggests that essays "hang somewhere on a line between two sturdy poles: this is what I think, and this is what I am"; "luck and play", says Theodor Adorno, "are essential to the essay"; comparing the forms of literature "with sunlight reflected in a prism", Georg Lukács concludes that essays are like "the ultraviolet rays".

III

THE HISTORY OF the Esse is easily told. It begins with a nineteenth-century Edinburgh-born entrepreneur, James Smith, who emigrated to America and settled in Jackson, Mississippi. There, he established a successful hardware business, specializing in cooking ranges and stoves. Business flourished, but Mississippi's climate had a detrimental effect on his wife's health, so they returned to Scotland. James's business acumen and the pool of wealthy customers in Victorian Edinburgh soon spelled success on that side of the Atlantic too. In 1858 he went into partnership with an old friend, Stephen Wellstood, and in 1890 Smith & Wellstood amalgamated with George Ure's

Colombian Stove Works at Bonnybridge in Stirlingshire, from whose foundry finished stoves were shipped down the Forth-Clyde canal to warehouses in Glasgow. Soon the business grew beyond Scotland. Outlets opened in Liverpool, Dublin and London. The first closed, anthracite-burning stoves were introduced to the British market in 1900. This was the type of stove to which the brand name "Esse" was given. According to documents in the National Library of Scotland, Smith & Wellstood were "the driving force in persuading the British public to invest in efficient, slow burning stoves in place of open fires". It's easy to think of history in terms of a few set-piece dramatic instances, to chart human progress by focusing on its violently eye-catching upheavals – wars, plagues, famines. But think how big a revolution was brokered by the Esse as people moved from open hearth to ironclad fire. The rhythms of everyday life for countless families were profoundly altered. Smith & Wellstood became a limited company in 1949. In 1973 they became part of Newman Industries. When this business collapsed in 1984 it was bought by Ouzledale Foundry. Esses are still made today at their foundry in Barnoldswick, Lancashire, a town that can trace its history back to the Vikings.

It pleases me to think that James Smith would have walked along the same Edinburgh street as I did, years later, carrying my copy of *Best American Essays 1989.* This book played as foundational a role in the development of my writing as Smith did in the development of the Esse. The bookshop where I bought it was on Princes Street,

Edinburgh's famous main thoroughfare, so it's almost certain Smith would have been there. This kind of coincidence fascinates me. For either of us to arrive at that particular node of time and space, each bearing the unique particularities of our histories, results from a maze of interconnections and possibilities so complex that mapping it beyond the crudest cartography defies the imagination. I'm reminded of Nietzsche's "all eternity was needed to make this one moment." This applies to *every* moment. Existence juggles with so many possible outcomes that it seems incredible the threads of the actual are ever spun, or that we become part of their fabric. Alternatives are always possible, ready to be woven up instead of us. Our precariousness comes into sharpest focus when we almost lose our place upon the unlikely brocade of being. What new pattern would have resulted if I'd stopped to tie a shoelace thirty years ago on the day a terrorist bomb exploded in a building I'd just walked past? James Smith was shipwrecked on a return trip to America in September 1854. How would the threads of history have changed if he'd not been rescued after three days perilously adrift in the Atlantic? "Esse" means "actual existence", from the Latin "to be". Our actual existence is about as far from being cast-iron as you can get. Our lives have much more about them of the Esse's shifting embers than of the stove itself. We are raked by circumstance, drawn into uncertain alignments as our brief embers touch and collide, face outcomes dictated by the unpredictable draft of time that governs the temperature of being.

The history of the essay is not so simple. Today's essays stem from a confluence of many tributaries. Their sources are not always clear, nor is it easy to map their meanderings or determine where one river of words merged with another in the great watercourse of prose in which our wordy species swims. From a Western perspective, Michel de Montaigne (1533-1592) is usually presented as the inventor of this form, with Francis Bacon (1561-1626) named as its originator in English – leading on to that famous duo of periodical essayists, Joseph Addison (1672-1719) and Richard Steele (1672-1729) – and from them, in various leaps and bounds (Johnson, Goldsmith, Lamb, Hazlitt, Carlyle, Thackeray, Stevenson, Belloc, Chesterton), to Woolf and Orwell, with whose contributions histories of this particular vein too often stop, as if the genre was now of merely historical interest. In fact this genealogy, whose rosary of famous names I've listed, is of dubious legitimacy. As Terence Cave has recently argued, there's a world of difference between Montaigne's "*essais*" and Lamb's "essays". I'm not at all convinced that the contemporary essay could trace its bloodline back to Addison and Steele, or that it would want to. I happily leave the detailed plotting of such family histories to others; I'm. more interested in writing essays than in tracing their ancestry. Like any family history, though, it will no doubt contain surprises – such as the fact that the so-called father of modern journalism and doyen of the English essay, Richard Steele, was an Irishman. His last earthly remains, coincidentally, lie not far from where I'm writing these words in rural, Welsh-speaking Wales.

Whatever conclusions we reach about the provenance of the essay, when we ponder its origin and development we need to remember that the Western perspective is only one, and the English essay is not its sole representative. In *The Chinese Essay* (2000), David Pollard includes examples from the work of essayists who lived centuries before Montaigne. Looking to the Classical world, we can also point to proto-essayists in figures like Cicero, Plutarch and Seneca. There are many national traditions of essay writing. The French essay, the English essay and the American essay are particularly rich seams in the deposits of this genre, but they are by no means the only ones. Scholars can identify key figures along the way and plot out how they've influenced each other, they can categorize essays into types – the personal essay, the nature essay, the medical essay and so on – but it's impossible to be sure in any overarching sense that's valid beyond the welter of subtraditions, when or where this form first emerged. It surely existed before it was so named, and did so simultaneously in different places in different forms. This is not a genre with any single point of origin. Though there are some crucially important wellsprings, most obviously Montaigne, who's to say which shard of prose, in which language, in which century constitutes the original ur-essay that set the standard for its descendants to follow? Following a set pattern is, in any case, alien to this genre. R. Lane Kauffmann refers to the "skewed path" that essays follow, and to their "unmethodical method". In the Preface to the *Encyclopedia of the Essay* (1997), edited by Tracy Chevalier, Graham Good talks about "the essay's multiplicity of forms", its "spontaneity, its unpredictability, its very lack of a system". He admits the impossibility of mapping it. This is a fugitive and unpredictable genre. It prefers the margins to the mainstream; it eschews conformity. It is more inclined to skepticism, dissent and heresy than to any literary orthodoxy. But always, "at the heart of the essay", as Graham Good stresses, "is the voice of the individual."

As an essayist, not an historian of the essay, still less a literary critic expert in this genre, I have two main concerns in any account given of it. First, that it makes clear how vigorous and varied the contemporary essay is, as evidenced, for example, in the now twenty volumes of Robert Atwan's *Best American Essays*. Secondly, that it dismisses the Edwardian stereotype in whose deathly grip essays too often languish even now. As Graham Good puts it – in his *The Observing Self: Rediscovering the Essay* (1988) – "essay" and "essayist" are terms that still act to:

> Conjure up the image of a middle-aged man in a worn tweed jacket in an armchair smoking a pipe by a fire in his private library in a country house somewhere in southern England, about 1910, maundering on about the delights of idleness, country walks, old wine and old books, blissfully unaware that he and his entire civilization are about to be swept away.

This type of essay — miles removed from the kind of writing being done in the genre today-is characterized by Ian Hamilton as the "something-about-next-to-nothing school" involving "virtuoso feats of pointless eloquence". These quaint period pieces should not be allowed to mask the possibilities such writing offers today. Unless the dead-wood of these outmoded connotations can be got rid of, "essay" just sounds tedious.

IV

THE ORIGIN OF the name "Esse" is unclear. No one seems to know who bestowed it, or why it was thought this palin-drome would suit a cast iron kitchen stove. It was written in italic script in raised silver letters on a red triangular nameplate affixed to the front of our Esse at Whiteways. Describing a rare 1888 edition of Smith & Wellstood's catalogue, librarians at Edinburgh's National Library of Scotland note that the company's anthracite-burning stoves "were modeled on a French design". The history section on the website of the current manufacturer of Esses, Ouzledale Foundry, suggests that "the French sounding name reflected the fashion at the time for continental style stoves." There are meanings for "esse" in Latin, German, Italian and Portuguese — but so far as I know it has no meaning in French. I'm not sure why Esses were so called. Perhaps James Smith or Stephen Wellstood remembered the Latin they would have learned at any nineteenth-century Scottish

school and thought the existential resonance of "to be" fitted
well with the elemental function of their stoves – for think
how much of being human involves clustering around fires,
as we warm ourselves, cook our meals, light the dark, listen
to each other's stories.

The origin of the name "essay" is clear enough. Here,
there's no doubt about the French connection. Montaigne's
great work, first published in 1580, was entitled *Essais de
Michel Montaigne* and constitutes the first use of "essai" to
describe a mode of writing. O. B. Hardison puts things into
useful context in his contribution to Alexander Butrym's
excellent collection, *Essays on the Essay* (1989). According
to Hardison:

> The word "essay" comes from the Old French "essai," de-
> fined by Partridge as "a trial, an attempt." From this mean-
> ing comes English "to essay" in the sense of "to make a
> trial or attempt." ... The word also comes into English via
> the Norman French "assaier," "to assay," meaning to try or
> test, as in testing the quality of mineral ore.

It remains uncertain how close a connection it's legitimate
to draw between Montaigne's endeavors and those of later
essayists. But it is undoubtedly the experimental nature of
the genre that gives it much of its appeal, the way it allows

one to try things out. It offers no set procedure. It is, rather, a style of wondering and wandering in prose that tolerates massive variation in length, in language and in subject matter. As Carl Klaus puts it, "The essay is an open form" which "gives a writer the freedom to travel in any direction."

v

TWO THICK BLACK pipes, each the circumference of a thigh, led from the back of the Esse and disappeared into the kitchen ceiling. From here they connected with a flue which ran to one of two chimneys on Whiteways' red-tiled roof. When the wind was in a certain direction and blowing hard, the draft that allowed the fire to burn could become so magnified that, on rare occasions, the hotplate glowed red hot. A silver towel rail ran across the front of the Esse. Just behind it, above the ovens, was a thermometer. Its thread of mercury was broken into several bits which never moved – the result of the stove once over-heating in a gale. Below the ovens was a shiny silver spout of unknown purpose. Whenever a dribble of water escaped from it – I only recall this happening a couple of times in all those years – it caused a level of consternation in my mother that seemed disproportionate to the tiny amount of liquid on the floor. Sometimes it seemed as if she – the chief tender of the stove and the person who cooked on it – was so attuned to its moods that her own were affected by it. Damp, windless days, when the draught was poor and the ovens slow, seemed to occasion similar lassitude in her; high temperatures on windy days made fiery outbursts likely.

The Esse had something of the nature of one of those massive iron bollards found in harbors to which ships are moored, holding them securely at the quayside. It was a heavy punctuation mark of the familiar, a potent ingredient in the sense of home. On those occasions when the whole family was away all day, my mother worried about getting back "for the Esse", so that its tending would not suffer interruption. The only time its fire was allowed to go out was when we were on holiday – our annual fortnight's stay in Donegal. When we got back, lighting the Esse was a priority. Until it was successfully done – a fiddly, smoky, uncertain business – it didn't feel as if we'd properly returned. The Esse's steady heat, its regular stoking, raking, and ash-emptying rituals, re-established our domestic routines and warmed away that luminal state of being neither away nor yet securely home.

Compared to the practical function of the Esse, the essay's usefulness may seem remote, even negligible. Though I like to think its wordy fires of meaning satisfy a need that's as important, if less pressing, than those the Esse catered for, I know how easy it is to denigrate the abstract by laying it alongside the concrete. The poet's calling can seem ridiculous indeed if set beside hunger and what a farmer does. The Esse kept us warm in those pre-central heating days, it heated our food, it allowed us to bathe in comfort. This was where my mother baked that inimitable Ulster wheaten bread whose smell and flavor was such a key component in the complicated machinery that generated our sense of belonging. Compared to such elemental things, essays may seem trifling distractions. What use is fiddling with words when a family is cold and hungry and needs hot food? Yet whilst it's easy to divide things into such disparate priorities, it would be a poor existence that didn't move beyond the satisfaction of our basic needs. Without the paths an essay can weave, the Esse – for all its usefulness – remains a mute, unsinging object.

Touch the Esse with the hand of the essay and all sorts of windows open up. It is cocooned in a delicate tracery of stories. Pull on one thread and it awakens the lives of those in foundry and warehouse, in canal barge and in shop, all the hands that touched this cube of iron. Pull on another thread and the ore from which the Esse was forged takes us back to the geological age when it was laid down in the earth. Or we can let its anthracite grow ancient forests in the mind and spark pictures of the vanished creatures whose tread fell upon the embryonic wood which, eons later, became the Esse's fuel. An essay can make the Esse transparent, its solidity can be changed into water as we feel the surge of the Atlantic swell that so nearly cost James Smith his life – three hundred people perished when the ship he was on, the US mail steamer *Arctic*, collided with another vessel in fog off Newfoundland. Or, closer to home

than that icy Atlantic water, an essay can conjure the water
of Boomer's Dam, only a mile or two from Whiteways,
and the trout fished from there and cooked to sizzling per-
fection in the Esse's oven. Essays allow us to find portals
of meaning and mystery in the objects that surround us.
Going through them we can feel the pulse of being sounding beyond the accustomed heartbeat of the quotidian.
Looking at how Northern Ireland descended into its dark
"Troubles", shattering the mercury of tolerance as the temperature of sectarian hatred soared beyond anything reason
was calibrated to measure, the essay lets us see the Esse as
the reassuring face of normality. It can remind us that in the
maelstrom of violence that sometimes made it seem as if all
of Ulster was a war zone, ordinary life continued, people
baked and ate and sat in comfortable rooms decrying the
barbarity burgeoning around them.

Another thread of meaning crackles into life if we look
at the person who installed the Esse at Whiteways in 1949,
shortly after the house was built. This thread loops back to
the religious wars in France which were so potent a factor in
Montaigne's decision to retreat to the seclusion of his cha-
teau and live quietly, away from the savagery of his times.
Our Esse was fitted by a plumber called John Refaussé (we
all pronounced it "Refossey"), a descendant of one of the
Huguenot refugees who fled religious persecution in France
to settle in this part of Ireland, bringing with them their
knowledge of linen manufacture – knowledge that was to
have a profound influence on so many Irish lives. The first
Refaussé arrived with the Williamite army in 1689. John

Refaussé's hands were trained to the metal of pipes and stoves, not muskets and swords, but what they wrought had far more impact on us than the actions of any soldier or gunman. The "Boomer" of Boomer's Dam sounds a second Huguenot note to set beside Refaussé. This stretch of water was named after another refugee family who settled in Lisburn's environs. Their original name, "Boullmer", was soon turned into "Boomer" on the no-nonsense local tongue, just as "Menuret" became "Menary", "Le Bas" became "Bass", "De Vaques" became "Devanny", "Deyermond" became "Dorman" and so on, this settling of odd-sounding names into forms more easy on the indigenous ear marking an acculturation so successful it soon became almost invisible. These Huguenots of Lisburn are a reminder of the fact that sectarian conflict is far from being unique to modern Ulster. Its unreasoning hatred, its demonizing of "the other", seems, alas, to be a characteristic of our species.

VI

LINKING ESSE and essay may seem unwarranted, a spurious connection forged between two things that really have nothing to do with each other. Surely they are mere homonyms, words that just happen to share identical sounds without any coincidence of sense. To take such accidental twinning further is to court absurdity. There is, of course, an element of contrivance in looking at one through the lens of the other – but, in the circumstances, what essayist

could resist some dalliance with such a pairing? Simple
play comes into it. Richard Chadbourne talks of "the element of *homo ludens* in the essay". Essaying the Esse is, in
part, the otter-pleasure of swimming in an unexpected rill
of language. The pooling of these words is an irresistible
invitation to jump in. Beyond the fun of verbal splashing,
though, the Esse-essay pairing has more serious dimen-
sions, both in terms of opening portals and as a means
of trying to understand some of the influences that have
shaped me.

In *Dreamthorp*, Alexander Smith suggests that "the
world is everywhere whispering essays." I'm drawn to such
whispering and the everyday epiphanies at which they seem
to hint. Being an essayist is, to some extent, just a case of
listening intently and transcribing what you hear – "one
need only be the world's amanuensis," says Smith. But is it
possible, I wonder, that a background of positive associa-
tions – the Esse's benign presence throughout childhood
– made me reach out to the essay, as if to an old and trusted
friend, when I encountered it all those years later? Perhaps
the genre held some subliminal allure as irresistible as the
aroma of freshly baked wheaten bread. Posing the question
of the Esse's possible influence sparks a wider question.
How far, really, do we understand what moves us, what
leads to our choosing one path in life rather than another,
what, in the end, makes us who we are? For all the rational
reasons I can advance to account for my writing, I'm not
sure why I write, or why, writing, I favor this particular
form. The smell of hot ash and the sound of oven doors

surface ambiguously in my mind as I contemplate these imponderables. All of us across the ages cluster around some fire, warming our bones and supping hot food, fearful of the encroaching night, of pain, of loneliness and death. Who knows, really, as we do so, what influences are laid down upon us and where we'll turn as we look for answers?

BIBLIOGRAPHIC ADDENDUM

In his great *Dictionary of the English Language*, Samuel Johnson famously described the essay as "a loose sally of the mind; an irregular indigested piece; not a regular and orderly composition". ("Sally" in this context means a leap, a setting forth, an excursion, an outburst of fancy, wit, etc.). *Irish Elegies* might be seen as a descendent of such loose sallies, representing one of the many styles into which this type of writing has evolved in the two and half centuries since Johnson formulated his definition. One of the characteristics of the essay is that it tends to avoid the scaffolding of scholarship – footnotes, bibliographies, technical jargon. These are more characteristic of the rigidities of academic articles than the free-ranging spirit of a "loose sally of the mind". Despite this, given the particular focus of "An Essay on the Esse", it seemed appropriate to include a bibliographic addendum listing works referred to. This might prove welcome to some readers; it is easily ignored by those who find it superfluous.

Writing in *The Idler* in 1759, four years after the first

edition of his *Dictionary*, Johnson identified "the multiplication of books" as "one of the peculiarities which distinguish the present age". He went on to speculate about whether, in the same way that a surfeit of laws can characterize a corrupt society, so an ignorant one might be marked by having many books. One hopes that the proliferation of books about the essay expresses a burgeoning of interest in this fascinating genre rather than any state of ignorance ...

Adorno, T.W. "The Essay as Form," translated by Bob Hullot-Kentor and Frederic Will. *New German Critique*, Vol. 32 (1984), pp. 151-171.

Atkins, G. Douglas. *Estranging the Familial: Towards a Revitalized Critical Writing*. University of Georgia Press, Athens: 1992.

Atwan, Robert (ed.). *The Best American Essays* (Published annually since 1986 with a different guest editor each year). Ticknor & Fields, New York: 1986-1993; Houghton Mifflin, Boston: 1994-present.

Butrym, Alexander J. (ed.). *Essays on the Essay*. University of Georgia Press, Athens: 1989.

Cave, Terence. *How to Read Montaigne*. Granta Books, London: 2007.

Chadbourne, Richard. "A Puzzling Literary Genre: Comparative Views of the Essay." *Comparative Literature Studies*, Vol. 20, no. 1 (1983), pp. 131-153.

Chevalier, Tracy (ed.). *Encyclopedia of the Essay*. Fitzroy Dearborn, Chicago and London: 1997.

Fakundiny, Lydia (ed.). *The Art of the Essay*. Houghton Mifflin, Boston: 1991.

Good, Graham. *The Observing Self: Rediscovering the Essay.* Routledge, London: 1988.

Hamilton, Ian (ed.). *The Penguin Book of Twentieth Century Essays.* Allen Lane/Penguin Press, London: 1999.

Hardison, O. B. "Binding Proteus: An Essay on the Essay," in Alexander Butrym (ed.), *Essays on the Essay.* University of Georgia Press, Athens: 1989, pp. 11-28.

Hoagland, Edward. *The Tugman's Passage.* Random House New York' 1982 ("What I Think, What I Am" is also reprinted in Carl Klaus et al. (eds.), *In Depth: Essayists for Our Time*).

Kauffmann, R. Lane. "The Skewed Path: Essaying as Un-methodical Method." *Diogenes,* Vol. 143 (1988), pp. 66-92 (also reprinted in Alexander Butrym (ed.), *Essays on the Essay*).

Klaus, Carl, Chris Anderson, and Rebecca Blevins Faery (eds.). *In Depth: Essayists for Our Time.* Harcourt, Brace, Jovanovich, New York: 1990.

Luckács, Georg. *Soul and Form,* translated by Anna Bostock (see in particular "On the Nature and Form of the Essay: A Letter to Leo Popper"). MIT Press, Cambridge, MA: 1974.

Montaigne, Michel de. *The Complete Works: Essays, Travel Journal, Letters,* translated by Donald M. Frame and with an Introduction bv Stuart Hampshire. Everyman's Library, London: 2003.

Pollard, David (tr. & ed.). *The Chinese Essay.* Hurst, London: 2000.

Smith, Alexander. *Dreamthorp: A Book of Essays Written in the Country.* Strahan, London: 1863.

ALSO OF POSSIBLE INTEREST

Atkins, G. Douglas. *Tracing the Essay: Through Experience to Truth*. University ofGeorgia Press, Athens: 2005.

Bates, Martha A. (ed.). *5 Years of the 4th Genre*. Michigan State University Press, East Lansing: 2006.

D'Agata, John (cd.). *The Next American Essay*. GraywolfPress St Paul MN: 2003.

Gross, John (ed.). *The Oxford Book of Essays*. Oxford University Press, Oxford: 1991.

Gutkind, Lee (ed.). *In Fact: The Best of Creative Nonfiction*. W. W. Norton, New York: 2005.

Hall, Donald (ed.). *The Contemporary Essay*. Bedford St Martins, Boston: 1995.

Lopate, Phillip (ed.). *The Art of the Personal Essay: An Anthology from the Classical Era to the Present*. Doubleday, New York: 1994.

Roorbach, Bill (ed.). *Contemporary Creative Nonfiction: the Art of Truth*. Oxford University Press, New York: 2001.

Root, Robert and Michael Steinberg (eds.). *The Fourth Genre: Contemporary Writers of/on Creative Nonfiction*. Longman, New York: 2001. ❧

STEVEN CHURCH

Auscultation

CHAMBER I

IN AUGUST 2007 we all waited to hear news of 6 miners
trapped 1500 feet underground by a massive cave-in at
the Crandall Canyon coal mine in Utah, a catastrophic
collapse so intense that it registered as a 3.9 magnitude
earthquake on seismographs. As rescuers began the ardu-
ous 3-day process of digging the men out, they also erected
seismic listening devices on the surface and set off 3 dy-
namite charges, a signal to any surviving miners to make
noise. Lots of noise. The electronic ears listened for the
sound of hammers pounding on the rock and on roof bolts,
the telltale rap-and-thump of human life. We listened and
listened but never heard a thing.

Six miners missing. Six boreholes drilled into different areas of the mine. They sent oxygen sensors, cameras,
and microphones down through PVC pipe, fishing in each
hole, searching every possible area for the men. Oxygen
levels were misread, confused, and ultimately determined
to be dangerously low. Three rescue workers trying to dig
the trapped miners out were also killed when a wall of the
mine "explodes", crushing them. We never saw or heard any

sign of the miners, and all 6 men were considered missing and presumed dead. All rescue efforts were eventually
abandoned. I don't know if there is a signal for this, another
series of blasts to say goodbye, or some other ceremonial
end to the search. Maybe they just switch off the drills and
unplug their ears.

The owner of the mine, Bob Murray held a press confer-
ence and said, "Had I known that this evil mountain, this
alive mountain, would do what it did, I would never have
sent the miners in here. I'll never go near that mountain
again."

Finally a seventh hole was bored into the mountain and
through this hole they pumped thousands of gallons of
mud and debris, filling all remaining cavities and sealing the
tomb off permanently with the missing miners still inside.

Researchers today at Utah State University are working
to create more effective listening and noise-making devices
to help trapped miners – some of them seemingly crude
and simplistic, yet still effective. One plan calls for 4 x 4 inch
iron plates to be placed at regular intervals in the tunnels,
with sledgehammers kept nearby – the idea being that a
trapped miner can find his way to a station and slam the
hammer into the iron plate over and over again. Think of
the noise below. Think of your ears. Geophones on the
surface – the kind of sensors they use to anticipate earth-
quakes – would register the sound waves created by the
hammer pings and create a listening grid, a kind of sound
map of the mine, which they would then use to pinpoint
the exact location of any miners still kicking below the
rugged skin.

CHAMBER 2

Recall the ice-cold press of the metal disc against your cavity, the sting and soft burn as it warms on your clavicle, your breastbone, fingers moving metal across your naked chest, around behind, fingertips stepping down your spine, one hand on your hip, maybe your shoulder, the other sliding around your rib-cage, always, always with the whispered command, *breathe . . . breathe . . . good*, and the eyes staring not at you but at the cold diaphragm, the metallic spot on your body, listening as if your body possesses a voice of its own and speaks in a language only others understand. The diaphragm will only broadcast its secret to the touch. It knows you. And when it touches you, it sings sounds of your body, noises you can barely imagine – the hypnotic pump of organs, the soft ebb and flow of blood in your veins, and the breathy whisper of lungs at work – noises that can name you *normal*, *healthy*, or *not*. The intimate instrument – the stethoscope – knows your body in a way your own hands and ears never can.

CHAMBER 3

Some heart doctors train their ears on classical music – Mozart and Bach and Chopin – learning to discern the individual instruments: to hear baritone from trombone, trumpet from sax, and the *tum-tum* of kettle over bongo or bass. They learn to listen for the flaws and failings of the heart, to recognize the music of machine-like muscle efficiency, and to understand when a noise is a bad noise. They depend on the stethoscope for more than diagnoses. They need it to be whole. Nothing promises Doctor like a stethoscope draped around an exposed neck or curled over a pressed, collared shirt, perhaps tucked neatly into the pocket of a white lab coat, or clutched firmly in hand, authoritatively like a craftsman's hammer, a plumber's seat wrench, or a surgeon's scalpel – the only tool for a specific job. You are familiar with the flexible latex tubing, the chrome-plated ear tubes, the hard metal diaphragm – cold, round, smooth as pearl, reflective as a mirror. The stethoscope immediately identifies a doctor – an icon of care and pain management, a reliquary of body knowledge, someone you trust with your life. Think of the things you've allowed another person to do and say to you, mainly because he wore the uniform of doctor and carried a stethoscope. We don't check resumes or credentials, don't ask for service reviews or certificates. We expect and accept the object. Even if it's never used (but it's always used), its appearance conjures a sense memory of that repeated sweet burn when pressed to your flesh. Regardless of physical context or attire (say at a crowded beach, in a subway, or on a mountain trail) the stethoscope speaks. It says, "I am a doctor," and in so doing it grants rights and responsibilities, obligations and expectations. It tells us you will do no harm. It tells us you know what you are talking about. Every child's Doctor play-set comes with a plastic stethoscope because you can't dress up as a doctor without one.

As object, it functions as both necessary and sufficient condition of "Doctorness". But this identity and image –

of the Doctor as listener, as diviner of significant sounds through a stethoscope, the magician of auscultation – is a relatively new one, just over 150 years old. The French doctor René Laennec is credited by many for inventing the first stethoscope, or at least for introducing the diagnostic practice of auscultation. In a paper published in 1819, he says:

> I was consulted by a young woman with symptoms of a diseased heart … percussion was of little avail on account … of fatness. The application of the ear … inadmissible by the age and sex of the patient. I recollected a fact in acoustics … the augmented sound conveyed through solid bodies.… I rolled a quire of paper into a cylinder and applied one end to the heart and one end to the ear … and thereby perceived the action of the heart … more clear and distinct. I have been enabled to discover new signs of the diseases of the lungs, heart and pleura.

It wasn't until the 1851 invention by Arthur Leared, and the refinement in 1852 by George Cammann, of the binaural stethoscope – a simple but incredibly significant instrument – that the practice of refined auscultation began to develop and doctors could listen in stereo to the sounds of the body. Before that it was a crude monaural amplifying horn, Laennec's ear-trumpet, which offered little more than a distant thump against the rib cage. Without binaural stethoscope technology, auscultation was more like listening for trees falling in a distant forest or miners tapping faintly in a deep pit. But doctors still pressed ears to chest cavities and listened for the pings, trying to read the heart's noises and tremors. L. A. Conner (1866-1950), the founder of the American Heart Association, is said to have carried a silk handkerchief to place on the wall of the chest for ear auscultation.

For 100 years cardiologists relied on Cammann's binaural scope to detect the slightest abnormality, arrhythmia, skip, hop, hammer, block or stutter. 1952 and 1964 saw further refinements of the traditional binaural stethoscope, with many cardiologists believing that the now all-but-obsolete Rapport-Sprague was the finest auscultation device ever made or used, allowing them unprecedented clarity and consistency.

Current research is focused on developing a reliable electronic amplified stethoscope, which is not actually a listening device but a noise translator that generates a reproduction of the heartbeat, bullying the human ear out of its place as the direct register of the heart.

I first heard the *whoosh-whoosh* of my daughter's heart as reproduction, as an electronic transmission through a fetal heart monitor strapped to my wife's belly – an electronic stethoscope. The sound is less a *thump* than a *slosh*. More valve and flap than muscled push. But it is still a treasured sound. For most of our prenatal visits, medical intervention extended only as far as placement of the fetal heart monitor. The first thing we did – doctor and parents – was listen. All together. We awaited the news of life. And anyone who's been in this place understands the simple comfort of that sound, the reassurance of that noise – or more directly, the doctor's recognition that this is *normal* noise.

A baby's heartbeat is the first sensory experience a father has with his child, often the first moment that a father begins to think of the fetus as a child. A baby: body and brain and lungs and drumming hearts. An identity: the first hint of possibility filtered through an electronic translator, reproduced from a tiny speaker. Nothing promises *person* like these first heart sounds. Nothing says, *it begins*, like the *wish-wish-wish* noise of the stubborn pump – and I say this with both knowledge and ignorance of the ethical implications for some.

Perhaps because of facts, stats, opinions, and ideas – or perhaps because I had no other way to feel my wife's pregnancy – fatherhood was mostly an abstraction. I never

really began to *feel* like a baby's father until I heard the
thumping inside, that tell-tale tapping. Or perhaps my
son was not a son, my daughter not a daughter, at least in
part, until their first heart noises registered in my ear – a
formation of identity that wasn't even possible when my
grandfather was born in 1906, or my father in 1945, and
was still only a rough science when I was born in 1971. But
I know that, in many ways, I did not identify myself as a
father until I heard my child's heart, and that I couldn't
have heard this without the aid of a stethoscope. Most of
us identify a doctor by the stethoscope, that intimate disc.
But it also identifies parent and child. All three fledgling
identities intertwine in that examination room, hopelessly
dependent on the curl and twisting turns of simple listening
technology, the only tool for the vital job of reading and
feeling the rhythmic thumps of the heart, that *tap-tap-tap*
signal of life we cannot see and I can in no other way sense.

CHAMBER 4

The year is 2002, and 9 coal miners are trapped in the
Quecreek Mine in Pennsylvania by rising water released
after a drilling machine punches through a wall into an
underground spring. The 9 men – a father and son among
the crew – retreat to the highest spot in the mine and rope
themselves together. They listen for the signal from the
surface – 3 small explosions – but don't hear anything.
They start pounding on the roof bolts with their ham-

mers, hoping to make some noise the surface can recognize. They pound and pound, but background noise on the surface interferes, and the seismic listening devices can't hear them. The men write notes to family members, seal them in a metal lunch box, and wait to die. As rescuers work frantically to pull water from the mine with massive diesel-powered pumps, they also drill down from the surface to pump oxygen into the cave where the rescuers hope the men have retreated. If the miners are alive, they can only be in one place, all of them protected by a small womb of air against the rising flood. The miners continue pounding on the roof bolts, but they get no response. The miners' families gather on the surface, huddled in a tent around the drill operator – because perhaps he is more than an operator and more than muscle: he's more like the human side of the machine, the listening side, the man with the touch, who watches the spin of metal, waiting. When the drill finally reaches the light-less room, 240 feet down, and punches like an amnio-needle into the pocket, the drill operator shuts off the machine, quiets the crowd, and listens. I wonder what it was that he listened for. How faint? How rhythmic? He listens, his hands on the machine, until he finally hears or feels the rhythmic noise of the trapped men hammering at the steel – the sole musical evidence of survival. Above them, on the outside, the expectant wives and mothers rejoice. They hug the man at the drill and slap each other on the back and think of how they can't wait to see and touch and smell their babies again. ❧

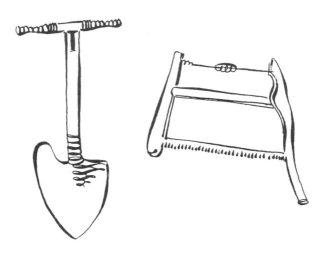

E. B. WHITE

The Practical Farmer[*]

MY PUBLISHERS HAVE PRESENTED ME with H. A. Highstone's book *Practical Farming for Beginners*, the sly inference being that I have much to learn. Publishers are on the whole well satisfied to have their writers disappear into rural circumstances, but they are genuinely concerned about how we put in our time. I am sure that, like parents whose children have left home, publishers are often visited with vague forebodings, sudden twinges of fear, the feeling that something is about to fall on writers — an eight-pound striking hammer perhaps, or a fit of loneliness.

There are ample grounds for this alarm. When a person who has been accustomed to making his living by writing attempts to combine this heavy work with the even heavier work of growing some of his own food, the consequences may be grave. If recent book lists are any indication, the country must be overrun with writers who are whipping their environment into shape for publication. The strain is very great, on both nature and man, and I sometimes wonder which will crack first. There is something ominous

---

*   From *One Man's Meat* (Harper & Bros., 1944).

about an impatient author, with a deadline to meet, keeping petulant vigil in a pumpkin patch so that he will be on time with his impressions of fall.

For me, always looking for an excuse to put off work, a farm is the perfect answer, good for twenty-four hours of the day. I find it extremely difficult to combine manual labor with intellectual, so I compromise and just do the manual. Since coming to the country I have devoted myself increasingly to the immediate structural and surgical problems that present themselves to any farmer, be he ever so comical in his methods and his designs. I have drifted farther and farther from my muse, closer and closer to my post-hole digger.

The blurb that accompanies *Practical Farming for Beginners* states that the book will be welcomed by "an increasing number of American people who, fed up with the pressure of city living, are going back to the land for their livelihood." That shows that publishers do not understand the situation. Pressure of city living? No pressure that I ever knew in town compares with the pressure of country living. Never before in my life have I been so pressed as in the past two years. Forty acres can push a man hard even when he isn't in debt, provided he loves them and is an easy victim to the stuff he reads in the bulletins. Pressure! I've been on the trot now for a long time and don't know whether I'll ever get slowed down. Today is our bean harvest, and even the beans in their screw-top jars are under pressure (ten pounds) in our new pressure canner, so hot are we to get them processed in one-third the time it might otherwise take. And when there is pressure up in the kitchen, it transmits itself to the whole place, and the tension becomes noticeable in all departments.

One morning a few months ago, during a particularly busy time, when I awoke I didn't dare get dressed: I knew that my only hope of getting an overdue piece written was to stay in bed – which is where I did stay. I told my wife it was a slight sore throat, but it was a simple case of voluntary confinement. It was the first time I had ever taken to bed in the full blush of health simply because I didn't dare face the economic consequences of putting my pants on.

Mr. Highstone's book presents a formula for subsistence farming, that is, farming for consumption rather than for profit, farming to produce *all* one's needs. It is the best diagram of that scheme I have studied. It is hardboiled, sound, persuasive, and convincing. On that account I regard it as one of the most dangerous of books, capable of destroying whole families, wiping them out like flies; for it suggests that any city man of average ability can create, within a couple of years and with his own hands, a satisfactory and secure economy based on the land, independent of any other source. This I do not believe. I believe that relatively few city-bred men are capable of achieving self-sufficiency through farming, and that, on the whole, the ones that might be capable of it wouldn't be particularly interested in it. Mr. Highstone is obviously a man with a gift for organization. He possesses a dauntless spirit, a keen financial sense, and the sort of mechanical ability that makes him jack-of-all-trades. He even writes well. He is informed, and he tells what he knows. His chapter called "The Chicken Trap" could only have been written by a man who had experienced the disappointments of an ill-planned poultry venture and who had learned to hate the very guts of a hen. It should certainly be read and digested by any person who dreams of lightening his old age by collecting eggs at sundown.

Briefly Mr. Highstone's formula is this:

To sustain yourself on the land, you must first get straight in your head that there is to be no nonsense about "making a profit." There is to be no buying of chicken feed by the bag and marketing of eggs by the dozen cases. You must simply create a farm that will produce, directly, everything you need including a small regular cash income (not profit). Any deviation from this course will get you into hot water. Furthermore, you must have enough capital at the start so that you won't be mortgaging your future. Mr. Highstone tells you how many thousands of dollars you will need to get started, how many acres you must buy (how many in grass, how many in grain, how many in gardens), and he names the animals you will need, the number of tons of every grain you must produce, the extra amount of cream and eggs you must sell to provide the monthly check, and the equipment you will need in house and barn. He faces life with confidence, and by the time you have read the book you, too, will face life with confidence and will believe that you can harness a team and hold a plow.

To create a self-sustaining farm, he says, you must have the following set-up:

Three cows.

One hundred hens (no more, no less).

A team of horses (which you buy after reading *Farmer's Bulletin 779*, "How to Select a Sound Horse").

Three or four hogs. (Usually Mr. Highstone is much more specific than this and says definitely three, or definitely four, but in this case there is a little leeway and you can decide between three hogs and four hogs.)

A hive of bees.

Enough land to grow all the feed for the above animals and for yourself and family, namely, ten tons of grain, fifteen tons of hay, and the usual vegetables and fruits. That's what you have to have. From these animals and this land you will receive all the food you and your family need, plus forty dollars a month – $25 from eggs, $15 from cream.

The principle on which this method of subsistence works is this:

The cow is the foundation on which the structure is built. The cow provides the means of producing, from the land, the indispensable commodities, milk, butter, and cheese. Furthermore the cow provides skim-milk, the by-product that makes diversification possible. Skim milk contains the protein that makes chickens lay eggs and makes hogs grow. This protein is ordinarily provided (on profit-and-loss farms) by expensive concentrates bought at a grain store – laying mash, hog ration, etc. Mr. Highstone will have you buy nothing, and he is very stern about that. It's forbidden, and if you start slipping and buy a bag of grain, your whole structure will topple. The cow also provides surplus cream, which is saleable and from which you get a monthly check, along with a check for the eggs that the hens laid because they were fed skim milk and that they wouldn't have laid if they had been on a straight grain diet.

The author admits that there is nothing new or original about this scheme; his contribution is in establishing the correct balance and in pointing out the fallacy of disturbing the balance by adding here or subtracting there. Thus the scheme fails, for instance, if the farmer reduces his hens to a flock of twelve or increases them to a flock of five hundred; twelve hens won't provide extra money from the sale of eggs, and five hundred hens will turn into a poultry farm and will take more time than a diversified farmer can give and will consume more food than he can raise on his property.

Mr. Highstone, being himself a practicing farmer, knows one important truth about country life: he knows that farming is about twenty per cent agriculture and eighty per cent mending something that has got busted. Farming is a sort of glorified repair job. This is a truth that takes some people years to discover, and many farmers go their whole lives without ever really grasping the idea. A good farmer is nothing more nor less than a handy man with a sense of humus. The repair aspect of farming looms so large that, on a place like my own, which is not really a farm at all but merely a private zoo, sometimes months go by when nothing but repair goes on. I can get so absorbed in the construction of a barn door that I can let the spring planting season go right by without ever opening the ground or sowing a seed. If I were engaged in making myself self-sustaining, I should perhaps be a little wider awake; but I know, from experience, that at any given moment of the year I would be found doing the wrong thing, and with a dull tool. I mention this because the weakness in Mr. Highstone's book is not in his plan for subsistence but in the people who are going to carry it out. In spite of all his warnings, there will be plenty of them who will get sidetracked, probably along the line of some special hobby, hitherto unindulged. I have been fooling around this place for a couple of years, but nobody calls my activity agriculture. I simply like to play with animals. Nobody knows this better than I do – although my neighbors know it well enough and on the whole have been tolerant and sympathetic.

Mr. Highstone wisely insists that the man who intends to get a living from the land begin not by studying agronomy but by learning to hollow-grind an ax and file a saw. He insists that you equip yourself, immediately, with dozens of tools and implements including a pipe vise, a drill press, a forge, and a 2-horse stationary gasoline engine. "The fact," says Mr. Highstone, "that a man may be unfamiliar with some of them should never daunt him" I have a strong suspicion, although I know nothing about Mr. Highstone, that his years in the city were spent dreaming not so much about fields of ripening grain as about a shop equipped with a pipe vise. The ecstatic passages in his book are not the ones dealing with husbandry and tillage but the ones dealing with edge tools. He demands that the subsistence farmer equip himself right at the start with four hundred dollars' worth of implements and tools, including a walking plow, a two-horse spike harrow, a one-horse row cultivator, a wire hayrake, a mowing machine, a buck rake, a stone boat, a farm wagon, a roller, a disk harrow, and a long list of tools ending with an assortment of nuts and bolts, washers, and wood screws. (Incidentally, he forgot a crowbar, a clawbar, a block-and-tackle, and a pair of tinner's snips, without which my own life would be empty indeed.)

In all this, and in fact in his pattern for a self-contained farm, he seems to me essentially sound. It is only in his assumption that a city man of average intelligence, strength, and will power can operate a self-contained farm that he appears fanciful. Some of the bald statements in his book are open to question. He says: "Anyone with brains enough to pound sand can successfully raise chickens." I think that is a misleading pronouncement. Raising chickens (except in very small quantities) is partly luck, partly experience, and partly a sort of gift, or talent.

In another place Mr. Highstone actually suggests that the subsistence family harvest its own grain crop by mowing it with a mowing machine and making sheaves by hand. Remember that the grain harvest is ten tons, or 200 sacks of grain each weighing one hundred pounds. And remember also that the grain harvest comes at the same season as the canning – those 600 Mason jars that have to be filled. It would take a large family of stalwart sons and daughters to put through that program without cracking. Some of the jars are going to crack even if the children don't.

The life of self-sufficiency in this 20th century is the dream of persons with a nostalgic respect for early

American vitality and ingenuity It conflicts, temperamentally, with modern ways. If I were to attempt I put myself on a self-sustaining basis I know that for practical reasons I would have to throw the master switch in the cellar and send my regrets to the Power Company, not simply because I couldn't afford to buy power on forty dollars a month but because the possession of power in the household leads on into paths that are inimical to self-sufficiency. They lead direct to the profit (and loss) system. Mr. Highstone devotes a section to the septic tank and sewage-disposal system; but my first step in the direction of security on the land would be to abandon all flush toilets, not because I don't approve of them but because they can destroy one's economy. People differ about plumbing. Mr. Highstone proposes to lick plumbing with a pipe vise. His is the manly approach. But I know my limitations. The practical way for me to lick plumbing is not to have any. I would also have to abandon my electric refrigerator, my electric water pump, my electric water heater, my electric lights, and I would have to sell my furnace and use the coal bin for storing root vegetables. There are days when I could take the leap with a glad cry; there are other days when I would hesitate.

The great service Mr. Highstone has rendered in his book is to clarify the scene. He tells what self-sufficiency means, tells where back-to-the-landers go wrong and how they confuse the idea of being self-sustaining with the idea of running a country business for profit. Of course even the most realistic subsistence farmers are sometimes wanderers in the paths of evil. I can picture the day in the Highstone family when the news got round that Father was writing a book called *Practical Farming for Beginners*. He started secretly, but writers give themselves away eventually, and pretty soon the family knew that something was up.

"What's Pop doing, Mom?" one of the little Highstones asked.

"Sh-h, he's writing a book, dear," replied Mrs. Highstone.

"You can't eat a book, Mom."

"Well, no-o. But you see your father will receive money from the sale of the book, and with the money we can buy what we need."

"What about that sauerkraut he was going to put up today?"

"He will soon have money so we can *buy* some sauerkraut."

"Will we have sugar in our coffee instead of honey?"

"Maybe."

"That's cheating, isn't it, Mom?"

"I wouldn't know, darling. Ask your father."

And so, above the Highstone farm, the specter of Profit raised its ugly head. ❧

JONATHAN FRANZEN

Scavenging*

(NOT MANY WAREHOUSES masquerade as châteaux, and of those that do, the Mercer Museum in Doylestown, Pennsylvania, is surely one of the largest. The museum is a hundred feet tall, has the flat face and square turrets of a reform school or a sandcastle, and is made entirely of poured concrete. A wealthy eccentric named Henry Mercer built it in the first decade of the century, in part as an advertisement for concrete and in part as housing for his unparalleled collection of the tools that American industrialization was rendering useless. Mercer had cruised the barns and auctions of his changing world and had brought back to Bucks County every imaginable style of cobbler's last, cider press and blacksmith's bellows, also a whaling launch complete with harpoons. In the museum's highest turret you'll find a trapdoor gallows and a horse-drawn hearse. Dozens of hand-carved sleds and cradles are stuck, as by poltergeist, to the vaulted concrete ceiling of the seven-story atrium.

The Mercer can be a very frosty place. Toward the end

---

*   From *How to be Alone: essays* (Picador, 2003).

of a visit on a recent December afternoon, I was devoting my most serious attention to the displays on the ground floor, where the heaters are. It was here that I encountered my own telephone, lodged in a glass case labeled OBSOLETE TECHNOLOGY.

My telephone is a basic black AT&T rotary, first leased from New England Bell in 1982, then acquired outright in the chaos of Ma Bell's breakup two years later. (I seem to recall not paying for it.) The Mercer's identical copy was perched uneasily on a heap of eight-track tapes – a pairing that I right away found hurtful. Eight-track tapes are one of the great clichés of obsolescence. A rotary phone, on the other hand, still served proudly in my living room. Not long ago I'd used it to order computer peripherals from the 408 area code, if you want to talk about modern.

The display at the Mercer was an obvious provocation. And yet the harder I tried to dismiss it, the more deeply I felt accused. I became aware, for example, of the repressive energy it was costing me to ignore my visits to the Touch-Tone in my bedroom, which I now relied on for account balances and flight information and train schedules. I became aware of additional energy spent on hating the voice-mail systems that relegate a rotary to second-class ("please hold for an operator") status. I became aware, in a word, of codependency. My rotary was losing its ability to cope with the modern world, but I continued to cover for it and to keep it on display downstairs, because I loved it and was afraid of change. Nor was it the only thing I protected in this way. I was suddenly aware of having a whole dysfunctional family of obsolete machines.

My TV set was a hulking old thing that showed only snow unless the extension-cord wire that served as an antenna was in direct contact with my skin. I wonder, is it possible to imagine a grimmer vision of codependency than the hundreds of hours I logged with sharp strands of copper wire squeezed between my thumb and forefinger, helping my TV with its picture? As for a VCR, it happened that the friend with whom I was visiting the Mercer had stepped off a plane from Los Angeles, the night before, with a VCR in a plastic shopping bag. He was giving it to me to make me stop talking about not having one.

I do still talk about not owning a CD player, and I pretend not to own any CDs. But for more than a year I've been finding myself in the houses of friends, in borrowed apartments, even in an artists-colony library, furtively making tapes of CD-only releases. Afterward I play the tapes on my tape deck and forget where they came from – until, in one of those squalid repetitions that codependency fosters, I need to convert another CD.

The display at the Mercer, on that cold December afternoon, was like a slap in the face from the modern world: *It was time to grow up.* Time to retire the rotary. Time to recall: Change is healthy. Accepting the inevitable is healthy. If you don't watch out, you'll be an old, old man at thirty-five.

As I write this, however, months later, my rotary phone is still in service. I've portrayed my appliances' obsolescence as a character defect of theirs for which I, like an addict's spouse, am trying to compensate. The truth is that the defect, the disease, inheres in me. The obsolescence is my own. It stems directly from what I do and don't do for a living.

At the root of both of my reasons for keeping the rotary is a fiction-writer's life.

One reason, the obvious one, is that while phones may be cheap, they're not free. As a fiction writer, pulling down a four-figure income, I'm the de facto inheritor of two hopelessly obsolete value systems: the Depression-era thrift of my parents' generation and the sixties radicalism of my older brothers' generation. People in the sixties were innocent enough to wonder: "Why should I work a job all week to pump more consumer dollars into a corrupt and dehumanizing system?" This is not a question you often hear asked anymore.

In his novel, *The Notebooks of Malte Laurids Brigge*, Rilke draws a parallel between the development of a poet and the history of Venice. He describes Venice as a city that has made something out of a nothing, as a city "willed in the midst of the void on sunken forests," a "hardened body, stripped to necessities," a "resourceful state, which bartered the salt and glass of its poverty for the treasures of the nations." Rilke himself was a paragon of mooching, the nonpareil of total avoidance of gainful employment, and he helped as much as anyone to shape my idea of what literature ought to be and of how a young writer might best achieve it. Fiction, I believed, was the transmutation of experiential dross into linguistic gold. Fiction meant taking up whatever the world had abandoned by the road and making something beautiful out of it.

Like one of those New Guineans who allegedly are unable to distinguish between a photograph and what is photographed, I spent my twenties literally combing weeds and Dumpsters and incinerator rooms for material, trying to make my life a more perfect metaphor for my art. The triumphant return home with scavenged loot – snow shovels, the business end of a broken rake, floor lamps, still-viable poinsettias, aluminum cookware – was as much a part of writing fiction as the typing up of final drafts. An old phone was as much a character in a narrative as an appliance in a home.

Thrift, then, literal and metaphoric, is one reason the rotary is still around. The other reason is that Touch-Tones repel me. I don't like their sterile rings, their plethora of features, their belatedness of design, the whole complacency of their hegemony. I prefer the reproachful heaviness of my rotary, just as I prefer the seventies clunkiness of my stereo components for the insult it delivers to the regiments of tasteful black boxes billeted in every house across the land.

For a long time, aesthetic resistance like this seemed valuable, or at least innocuous. But one day I wake up and find I've been left behind by *everyone*. One day the beauty of thrift and the ideal of simplicity end up petrified into barren, time-devouring obsessions. One day the victim of the market turns out to be not a trivial thing, like a rotary phone or a vinyl disc, but a thing of life-and-death importance to me, like the literary novel. One day at the Mercer it's not my telephone but my copies of Singer and Gaddis and O'Connor that are piled on top of eigh-tracks with inflammatory carelessness ("OBSOLETE TECHNOLOGY, OR: THE JUDGMENT OF THE MARKET"), as on the ash-heap of history. One day I visit the Mercer, and the next day I wake up depressed.

For six years the antidepressant drug Prozac has been lifting the spirits of millions of Americans and thousands of Eli Lilly shareholders.
　　　　　—*lead sentence of a* New York Times *story, January 9, 1994*

IT'S HEALTHY to adjust to reality. It's healthy, recognizing that fiction such as Proust and Faulkner wrote is doomed, to interest yourself in the victorious technology, to fashion a niche for yourself in the new information order, to discard and then forget the values and methods of literary modernism which older readers are too distracted and demoralized to appreciate in your work and which younger readers, bred on television and educated in the new orthodoxy of identity politics and the reader's superiority to the text, are almost entirely deaf and blind to. It's healthy to stop giving yourself ulcers and migraines doing demanding work that may please a few harried peers but otherwise instills unease or outright resentment in would-be readers. It's healthy to cry uncle when your bone's about to break. Likewise healthy, almost by definition, to forget about death in order to live your life: healthy to settle for (and thereby participate in) your own marginalization as a writer, to accept as inevitable a shrinking audience, an ever-deteriorating relationship with the publishing conglomerates, a retreat into the special Protective Isolation Units that universities now provide for writers. Healthy to slacken your standards, to call "great" what five years ago you might have called "decent but nothing special." Healthy, when you discover that your graduate writing students can't distinguish between "lie" and "lay" and have never read Jane Austen, not to rage or agitate but simply bite the bullet and do the necessary time-consuming teaching. Healthier yet not to worry about it – to nod and smile in your workshops and let sleeping dogs lay, let the students discover Austen when Merchant and Ivory film her.

In describing as "healthy" these responses to the death sentence obsolescence represents, I'm being no more than halfway ironic. Health really is the issue here. The pain of consciousness, the pain of knowing, grows apace with the information we have about the degradation of our planet and the insufficiency of our political system and the incivility of our society and the insolvency of our treasury and the injustice in the one-fifth of our country and four-fifths of our world that isn't rich like us. Given this increasing pain, it's understandable that a large and growing segment of the population should take comfort in the powerful narcotics that technology offers. The more popular these narcotics become, the more socially acceptable their use – and the lonelier the tiny core of people who are temperamentally incapable of deluding themselves that the "culture" of technology is anything but a malignant drug. It becomes a torture each time you see a friend stop reading books, and each time you read of another cheerful young writer doing

TV in book form. You become depressed. And then you see what technology can do for those who become depressed. It can make them undepressed. *It can bring them health.* And this is the moment at which I find myself: I look around and see absolutely everyone (or so it seems) finding health. They enjoy their television and their children and they don't worry inordinately. They take their Prozac and are undepressed. They are all civil with each other and smile undepressed smiles, and they look at me with eyes of such pure opacity that I begin to doubt myself. I seem to myself a person who shrilly hates health. I'm only a phone call away from asking for a prescription of my own ...)

SO ENDS THE FRAGMENT of essay that I've scavenged in assembling this one. I wrote the fragment two years ago when I was alone and unable to write fiction – unable, almost, to read a newspaper, the stories depressed me so much. The world hasn't changed much in the last two years, but I feel as if I have. Who knows if I can generalize from my own experience. All I know is that, soon after I wrote that fragment, I gave up. Just plain gave up. No matter what it cost me, I didn't want to be unhappy anymore. And so I stopped trying to be a writer-with-a-capital-W. Just to desire to get up in the morning was all I asked.

And then it was as if I began to remember. I remembered that as a boy I had spent long Saturday hours extracting rusty nails from the piles of paneling my father had torn out in the basement. I remembered hammering them straight on the piece of scrap iron my father had scavenged for an anvil, and then watching my father reuse these nails as he built himself a workshop and repaneled the basement. I remembered my adolescent adoration of my older brother Tom, who for a while in the seventies was an avant-garde filmmaker in Chicago, and who rehabbed an apartment in Pilsen with tools and materials largely scrounged from the now-defunct Maxwell Street market. Tom had two old Karmann Ghias, a bad yellow one handed down from our other brother, Bob, and an even worse pale blue one that had cost Tom one hundred fifty dollars. He alternately cannibalized each to feed the other; it was very time-consuming. I was riding with him the day the yellow one threw a rod and died and also the day the hood of the blue one blew open on the Dan Ryan Expressway and blocked the windshield. I clearly remember wishing to be nowhere in the world but standing next to Tom on the muffler- and tailpipe-strewn shoulder as he wired the Ghia's hood back into place.

When I began to write seriously in college, I used a hulking black Remington that rose nearly a foot off my desk, weighed as much as a small airconditioner, and took all my carpal strength to operate. Later, I wrote my first novel and half of my second on two portable Silver-Reed typewriters (fifty dollars in 1980, still only sixty-nine dollars in 1985). When they broke, I fixed them. A triumph, in a week when various journals returned five short stories with rejection letters, was my substitution of dental floss for the nylon cord that supplied carriage-advancing tension.

For typing up clean drafts, my wife and I shared a forty-pound electric Smith-Corona. Our old Chevy Nova was strictly a fair-weather friend, and it always seemed to be snowing when the Smith-Corona broke down. In the early eighties, in Boston, snow would pile up in drifts that my wife and I would struggle over, bundled like peasants as we half-dragged and half-carried the Smith-Corona to the Harvard Coop. Somewhere in the Coop's bowels dwelt a man named Mr. Palumbo. I never met Mr. Palumbo face to face, but we spoke on the telephone often. He had a raspy voice and you knew he was up to his elbows in machine oil. Mr. Palumbo loved the inexpensive fix, and I loved him for loving it. Once, on one of those prematurely indigo late afternoons that descend on Boston, he called to tell me that the main shaft had broken off the Smith-Corona's motor and that the motor would have to be replaced, at a cost of fifty dollars. It was obvious that he hated to have to tell me this. An hour or two later, well after nightfall, he called me again. "I fixed it!" he shouted. "I *glued* it. I *epoxy-glued* the shaft back on the motor!" As I recall, he charged us eighteen dollars for this service.

I bought my first computer in 1989. It was a noisy metal box made by Amdek. In good codependent form, I came to appreciate the noise of the Amdek's fan's hum. I told myself I liked the way it cut out the noise from the street and other apartments. But after about two years of heavy use the Amdek developed a new, frictive squeal whose appearance and disappearance seemed to follow the rise and fall of the air's relative humidity. My first solution was to wear earplugs on muggy days. After six months of earplugs, however, with the squeal becoming more persistent, I removed the computer's sheet-metal casing. Then the squeal stopped for no reason, and for several days I wrote fiction on a topless machine, its motherboard exposed. When the squeal returned, I discovered that I could make it stop by applying pressure to the printed-circuit board that controlled the hard disk. There was a space that I could wedge a pencil into, and if I torqued the pencil with a rubber band, the corrective pressure held. The cover of the computer didn't fit right when I put it back on; I stripped the threads off a screw and had to leave one corner of the cover sort of flapping.

To some extent, of course, everyone who is less than wealthy learns to cope with ailing equipment. Some of us are simply more vain about our coping. But it's not simply for their affirmation of my nature that I value my memories of writing prose on half-broken machines. The image of my decrepit but still-functional Amdek is also, for me, an image of America's enduring *raggedness*. Obsolescence is the leading product of our national infatuation with technology, and I now believe that obsolescence is not a darkness but a beauty: not perdition but salvation. The more headlong the progress of technological development, the greater the volume of obsolete detritus. And the detritus isn't simply material. It's angry religion, resurgent countercultural ideologies, the newly unemployed, the eternally unemployable. These are the fiction writer's guarantee that he or she will never be alone. Obsolescence is our legacy.

Because imaginative writing is fundamentally amateur. It's the lone person scouring the trash heap, not the skilled team assembling an entertainment, and we Americans are lucky enough to live in the most wonderful world of junk. Once, when I lived in Munich, I stole two cobblestones from a sidewalk construction site. I intended to wrap them in newspaper and make bookends. It was a Saturday afternoon, the streets were empty, and yet my theft seemed so terribly, terribly transgressive that I ran for blocks, a stone in each hand, before I was sure I was safe. And still I felt the stern eye of the State on me. Whereas in New York, where I now live, the Dumpsters practically *invite* me to relieve them of their useful bricks and lumber. Street people share lore with me over curbside dumps at midnight, under streetlamps. In the wee hours they spread their finds on soiled quilts at the corner of Lexington and 86th Street and barter dubious clock-radios for chipped glass doorknobs. Use and abandonment are the aquifer through which consumer objects percolate, shedding the taint of mass production and emerging as historied individuals.

It's tempting to imagine the American writer's resistance to technoconsumerism – a resistance which unfortunately in most cases takes the form of enforced economic hardship – as some kind of fungible political resistance. Not long ago, one of my former undergraduate workshop students came to visit, and I took him on a walk in my neighborhood. Jeff is a skilled, ambitious young person, gaga over Pynchon's critique of technology and capitalism, and teetering between pursuing a PH D in English and trying his

hand at fiction. On our walk, as I was ranting at him, telling
him that fiction is about refuge, not about social change,
we passed a delicous trash pile. There was a paint- and
plaster-spattered wooden chair with a broken seat, and I
found a scrap of two-by-four to knock the bigger clumps
of plaster off. It was grubby work. Jeff said: "This is what
my life will be like if I write fiction?"

After years of depression, I didn't care how forgiving of
myself I sounded. I said that what mattered to me was the
rescue. I could probably afford a new chair; that I prefer
to live among the scavenged and reborn is my own private
choice.

A sponge bath, a scrap of sturdy ash plywood from a
dresser drawer abandoned at curbside, eight scavenged
brass screws to attach the plywood to the underside of
the seat, and a black magic marker to mask the spatters of
white paint: this is how the chair was rescued. ◝

Mowing

There was never a sound beside the wood but one,
And that was my long scythe whispering to the ground.
What was it it whispered? I knew not well myself;
Perhaps it was something about the heat of the sun,
Something, perhaps, about the lack of sound –
And that was why it whispered and did not speak.
It was no dream of the gift of idle hours,
Or easy gold at the hand of fay or elf:
Anything more than the truth would have seemed too weak
To the earnest love that laid the swale in rows,
Not without feeble-pointed spikes of flowers
(Pale orchises), and scared a bright green snake.
The fact is the sweetest dream that labor knows.
My long scythe whispered and left the hay to make.

—Robert Frost
A Boy's Will (1915)

HILAIRE BELLOC

The Mowing of a Field*

THERE IS A VALLEY in South England remote from ambition and from fear, where the passage of strangers is rare and unperceived, and where the scent of the grass in summer is breathed only by those who are native to that unvisited land. The roads to the Channel do not traverse it; they choose upon either side easier passes over the range. One track alone leads up through it to the hills, and this is changeable: now green where men have little occasion to go, now a good road where it nears the homesteads and the barns. The woods grow steep above the slopes; they reach sometimes the very summit of the heights, or, when they cannot attain them, fill in and clothe the combes. And, in between, along the floor of the valley, deep pastures and their silence are bordered by lawns of chalky grass and the small yew trees of the Downs.

The clouds that visit its sky reveal themselves beyond the one great rise, and sail, white and enormous to the other, and sink beyond that other. But the plains above which they have travelled and the Weald to which they go, the people of the valley cannot see and hardly recall.

---

* From *Hills and the Sea* (Methuen, 1906).

The wind, when it reaches such fields, is no longer a gale from the salt, but fruitful and soft, an inland breeze; and those whose blood was nourished here feel in that wind the fruitfulness of our orchards and all the life that all things draw from the air.

In this place, when I was a boy, I pushed through a fringe of beeches that made a complete screen between me and the world, and I came to a glade called No Man's Land. I climbed beyond it, and I was surprised and glad, because from the ridge of that glade I saw the sea. To this place very lately I returned.

The many things that I recovered as I came up the countryside were not less charming than when a distant memory had enshrined them, but much more. Whatever veil is thrown by a longing recollection had not intensified nor even made more mysterious the beauty of that happy ground; not in my very dreams of morning had I, in exile, seen it more beloved or more rare. Much also that I had forgotten now returned to me as I approached – a group of elms, a little turn of the parson's wall, a small paddock beyond the graveyard close, cherished by one man, with a low wall of very old stone guarding it all around. And all these things fulfilled and amplified my delight, till even the good vision of the place, which I had kept so many years, left me and was replaced by its better reality. "Here," I said to myself, "is a symbol of what some say is reserved for the soul: pleasure of a kind which cannot be imagined save in a moment when at last it is attained."

When I came to my own gate and my own field, and had before me the house I knew, I looked around a little

(though it was already evening), and I saw that the grass
was standing as it should stand when it is ready for the
scythe. For in this, as in everything that a man can do –
of those things at least which are very old – there is an
exact moment when they are done best. And it has been
remarked of whatever rules us that it works blunderingly,
seeing that the good things given to man are not given at
the precise moment when they would have filled him with
delight. But, whether this be true or false, we can choose
the just turn of the seasons in everything we do of our own
will, and especially in the making of hay. Many think that
hay is best made when the grass is thickest; and so they
delay until it is rank and in flower, and has already heavily
pulled the ground. And there is another false reason for
delay, which is wet weather. For very few will understand
(though it comes year after year) that we have rain always
in South England between the sickle and the scythe, or
say just after the weeks of east wind are over. First we have
a week of sudden warmth, as though the south had come
to see us all; then we have the weeks of east and southeast
wind; and then we have more or less of that rain of which
I spoke, and which always astonishes the world. Now it is
just before, or during, or at the very end of that rain – but
not later – that grass should be cut for hay. True, upland
grass, which is always thin, should be cut earlier than the
grass in the bottoms and along the water meadows; but not
even the latest, even in the wettest seasons, should be left
(as it is) to flower and even to seed. For what we get when
we store our grass is not a harvest of something ripe, but a
thing just caught in its prime before maturity: as witness

that our corn and straw are best yellow, but our hay is best green. So also Death should be represented with a scythe and Time with a sickle; for Time can take only what is ripe, but Death comes always too soon. In a word, then, it is always much easier to cut grass too late than too early; and I under that evening and come back to these pleasant fields, looked at the grass and knew that it was time. June was in full advance; it was the beginning of that season when the night has already lost her foothold of the earth and hovers over it, never quite descending, but mixing sunset with the dawn.

Next morning, before it was yet broad day, I awoke, and thought of the mowing. The birds were already chattering in the trees beside my window, all except the nightingale, which had left and flown away to the Weald, where he sings all summer by day as well as by night in the oaks and the hazel spinneys, and especially along the little river Adur, one of the rivers of the Weald. The birds and the thought of the mowing had awakened me, and I went down the stairs and along the stone floors to where I could find a scythe; and when I took it from its nail, I remembered how, fourteen years ago, I had last gone out with my scythe, just so, into the fields at morning. In between that day and this were many things, cities and armies, and a confusion of books, mountains and the desert, and horrible great breadths of sea.

When I got out into the long grass the sun was not yet risen, but there were already many colours in the eastern sky, and I made haste to sharpen my scythe, so that I might get to the cutting before the dew should dry. Some say that it is best to wait till all the dew has risen, so as to get the grass quite dry from the very first. But, though it is an advantage to get the grass quite dry, yet it is not worth while to wait till the dew has risen. For, in the first place, you lose many hours of work (and those the coolest), and next – which is more important – you lose that great ease and thickness in cutting which comes of the dew. So I at once began to sharpen my scythe.

There is an art also in the sharpening of a scythe, and it is worth describing carefully. Your blade must be dry, and that is why you will see men rubbing the scythe-blade with grass before they whet it. Then also your rubber must be quite dry, and on this account it is a good thing to lay it on your coat and keep it there during all your day's mowing. The scythe you stand upright, with the blade pointing away from you, and put your left hand firmly on the back of the blade, grasping it: then you pass the rubber first down one side of the blade-edge and then down the other, beginning near the handle and going on to the point and working quickly and hard. When you first do this you will, perhaps, cut your hand; but it is only at first that such an accident will happen to you.

To tell when the scythe is sharp enough this is the rule. First the stone clangs and grinds against the iron harshly; then it rings musically to one note; then, at last, it purrs as though the iron and stone were exactly suited. When you hear this, your scythe is sharp enough; and I, when I heard it in that June dawn, with everything quite silent except the birds, let down the scythe and bent myself to mow.

When one does anything anew, after so many years, one

fears very much for one's trick or habit. But all things once learnt are easily recoverable, and I very soon recovered the swing and power of the mower. Mowing well and mowing badly – or rather not mowing at all – are separated by very little; as is also true of writing verse, of playing the fiddle, and of dozens of other things, but of nothing more than of believing. For the bad or young or untaught mower without tradition, the mower Promethean, the mower original and contemptuous of the past, does all these things: He leaves great crescents of grass uncut. He digs the point of the scythe hard into the ground with a jerk. He loosens the handles and even the fastening of the blade. He twists the blade with his blunders, he blunts the blade, he chips it, dulls it, or breaks it clean off at the tip. If any one is standing by he cuts him in the ankle. He sweeps up into the air wildly, with nothing to resist his stroke. He drags up earth with the grass, which is like making the meadow bleed. But the good mower who does things just as they should be done and have been for a hundred thousand years, falls into none of these fooleries. He goes forward very steadily, his scythe-blade just barely missing the ground, every grass falling; the swish and rhythm of his mowing are always the same.

So great an art can only be learnt by continual practice; but this much is worth writing down, that, as in all good work, to know the thing with which you work is the core of the affair. Good verse is best written on good paper with an easy pen, not with a lump of coal on a whitewashed wall. The pen thinks for you; and so does the scythe mow for you if you treat it honourably and in a manner that makes it recognize its service. The manner is this. You must regard the scythe as a pendulum that swings, not as a knife that cuts. A good mower puts no more strength into his stroke than into his lifting. Again, stand up to your work. The bad mower, eager and full of pain, leans forward and tries to force the scythe through the grass. The good mower, serene and able, stands as nearly straight as the shape of the scythe will let him, and follows up every stroke closely, moving his left foot forward. Then also let every stroke get well away. Mowing is a thing of ample gestures, like drawing a cartoon. Then, again, get yourself into a mechanical and repetitive mood: be thinking of anything at all but your mowing, and be anxious only when there seems some interruption to the monotony of the sound. In this mowing should be like one's prayers – all of a sort and always the same, and so made that you can establish a monotony and work them, as it were, with half your mind: that happier half, the half that does not bother.

In this way, when I had recovered the art after so many years, I went forward over the field, cutting lane after lane through the grass, and bringing out its most secret essences with the sweep of the scythe until the air was full of odors. At the end of every lane I sharpened my scythe and looked back at the work done, and then carried my scythe down again upon my shoulder to begin another. So, long before the bell rang in the chapel above me – that is, long before six o'clock, which is the time for the *Angelus* – I had many swathes already lying in order parallel like soldiery; and the high grass yet standing, making a great contrast with the shaven part, looked dense and high. As it says in the *Ballad of Val-ès-Dunes*, where

> The tall son of the Seven Winds
> Came riding out of Hither-hythe,

and his horse-hoofs (you will remember) trampled into the press and made a gap in it, and his sword (as you know)

> … was like a scythe
> In Arcus when the grass is high
> And all the swathes in order lie,
> And there's the bailiff standing by
> A-gathering of the tithe.

So I moved all that morning, till the houses awoke in the valley, and from some of them rose a little fragrant smoke, and men began to be seen. I stood still and rested on my scythe to watch the awakening of the village, when I saw coming up to my field a man whom I had known in older times, before I had left the Valley.

He was of that dark silent race upon which all the learned quarrel, but which, by whatever meaningless name it may be called – Iberian, or Celtic, or what you will – is the permanent root of all England, and makes England wealthy and preserves it everywhere, except perhaps in the Fens and in a part of Yorkshire. Everywhere else you will find it active and strong. These people are intensive; their thoughts and their labours turn inward. It is on account of their presence in these islands that our gardens are the richest in the world. They also love low rooms and ample fires

and great warm slopes of thatch. They have, as I believe, an
older acquaintance with the English air than any other of
all the strains that make up England. They hunted in the
Weald with stones, and camped in the pines of the green-
sand. They lurked under the oaks of the upper rivers, and
saw the legionaries go up, up the straight paved road from
the sea. They helped the few pirates to destroy the towns,
and mixed with those pirates and shared the spoils of the
Roman villas, and were glad to see the captains and the
priests destroyed. They remain; and no admixture of the
Frisian pirates, or the Breton, or the Angevin and Norman
conquerors, has very much affected their cunning eyes.

To this race, I say, belonged the man who now approached me. And he said to me, "Mowing?" And I answered, "Ar." Then he also said "Ar," as in duty bound; for so
we speak to each other in the Stenes of the Downs.

Next he told me that, as he had nothing to do, he would
lend me a hand; and I thanked him warmly, or, as we say,
"kindly." For it is a good custom of ours always to treat bar-
gaining as though it were a courteous pastime; and though
what he was after was money, and what I wanted was his
labour at the least pay, yet we both played the comedy that
we were free men, the one granting a grace and the other
accepting it. For the dry bones of commerce, avarice and
method and need, are odious to the Valley; and we cover
them up with a pretty body of fiction and observances.
Thus, when it comes to buying pigs, the buyer does not
begin to decry the pig and the vendor to praise it, as is
the custom with lesser men; but tradition makes them do
business in this fashion: –

First the buyer will go up to the seller when he sees
him in his own steading, and, looking at the pig with admiration, the buyer will say that rain may or may not fall,
or that we shall have snow or thunder, according to the
time of the year. Then the seller, looking critically at the
pig, will agree that the weather is as his friend maintains.
There is no haste at all; great leisure marks the dignity of
their exchange. And the next step is, that the buyer says:
"That's a fine pig you have there, Mr. – " (giving the seller's
name). "Ar, powerful fine pig." Then the seller, saying also
"Mr." (for twin brothers rocked in one cradle give each other
ceremonious observance here), the seller, I say, admits, as
though with reluctance, the strength and beauty of the
pig, and falls into deep thought. Then the buyer says, as
though moved by a great desire, that he is ready to give so
much for the pig, naming half the proper price, or a little
less. Then the seller remains in silence for some moments;
and at last begins to shake his head slowly, till he says: "I
don't be thinking of selling the pig, anyways." He will also
add that a party only Wednesday offered him so much
for the pig – and he names about double the proper price.
Thus all ritual is duly accomplished; and the solemn act is
entered upon with reverence and in a spirit of truth. For
when the buyer uses this phrase: "I'll tell you what I *will* do,"
and offers within half a crown of the pig's value, the seller
replies that he can refuse him nothing, and names half a
crown above its value; the difference is split, the pig is sold,
and in the quiet soul of each runs the peace of something
accomplished.

Thus do we buy a pig or land or labour or malt or lime,

always with elaboration and set forms; and many a London man has paid double and more for his violence and his greedy haste and very unchivalrous higgling. As happened with the land at Underwaltham, which the mortgagees had begged and implored the estate to take at twelve hundred, and had privately offered to all the world at a thousand, but which a sharp direct man, of the kind that makes great fortunes, a man in a motor-car, a man in a fur coat, a man of few words, bought for two thousand three hundred before my very eyes, protesting that they might take his offer or leave it; and all because he did not begin by praising the land.

Well then, this man I spoke of offered to help me, and he went to get his scythe. But I went into the house and brought out a gallon jar of small ale for him and for me; for the sun was now very warm, and small ale goes well with mowing. When we had drunk some of this ale in mugs called "I see you," we took each a swathe, he a little behind me because he was the better mower; and so for many hours we swung, one before the other, mowing and mowing at the tall grass of the field. And the sun rose to noon and we were still at our mowing; and we ate food, but only for a little while, and we took again to our mowing. And at last there was nothing left but a small square of grass, standing like a square of linesmen who keep their formation, tall and unbroken, with all the dead lying around them when the battle is over and done.

Then for some little time I rested after all those hours; and the man and I talked together, and a long way off we heard in another field the musical sharpening of a scythe.

The sunlight slanted powdered and mellow over the breadth of the valley; for day was nearing its end. I went to fetch rakes from the steading; and when I had come back the last of the grass had fallen, and all the field lay flat and smooth, with the very green short grass in lanes between the dead and yellow swathes.

These swathes we raked into cocks to keep them from the dew against our return at daybreak; and we made the cocks as tall and steep as we could, for in that shape they best keep off the dew, and it is easier also to spread them after the sun has risen. Then we raked up every straggling blade, till the whole field was a clean floor for the tedding and the carrying of the hay next morning. The grass we had mown was but a little over two acres; for that is all the pasture on my little tiny farm.

When we had done all this, there fell upon us the beneficent and deliberate evening; so that as we sat a little while together near the rakes, we saw the valley more solemn and dim around us, and all the trees and hedgerows quite still, and held by a complete silence. Then I paid my companion his wage, and bade him a good night, till we should meet in the same place before sunrise.

He went off with a slow and steady progress, as all our peasants do, making their walking a part of the easy but continual labour of their lives. But I sat on, watching the light creep around towards the north and change, and the waning moon coming up as though by stealth behind the woods of No Man's Land. ๛

PHYLLIS ROSE

Tools of Torture[*]

IN A GALLERY off the rue Dauphine, near the *parfumerie* where I get my massage, I happened upon an exhibit of medieval torture instruments. It made me think that pain must be as great a challenge to the human imagination as pleasure. Otherwise there's no accounting for the number of torture instruments. One would be quite enough. The simple pincer, let's say, which rips out flesh. Or the head crusher, which breaks first your tooth sockets, then your skull. But in addition I saw tongs, thumbscrews, a rack, a ladder, ropes and pulleys, a grill, a garrote, a Spanish horse, a Judas cradle, an iron maiden, a cage, a gag, a strappado, a stretching table, a saw, a wheel, a twisting stork, an inquisitor's chair, a breast breaker, and a scourge. You don't need complicated machinery to cause incredible pain. If you want to saw your victim down the middle, for example, all you need is a slightly bigger than usual saw. If you hold the victim upside down so that the blood stays in his head, hold his legs apart, and start sawing at the groin, you can get as far as the navel before he loses consciousness.

---

* From *Never Say Goodbye* (Doubleday, 1991).

Even in the Middle Ages, before electricity, there were
many things you could do to torment a person. You could
tie him up in an iron belt that held the arms and legs up to
the chest and left no point of rest, so that all his muscles
went into spasm within minutes and he was driven mad
within hours. This was the twisting stork, a benign-looking
object. You could stretch him out backward over a thin
piece of wood so that his whole body weight rested on his
spine, which pressed against the sharp wood. Then you
could stop up his nostrils and force water into his stomach
through his mouth. Then, if you wanted to finish him off,
you and your helper could jump on his stomach, causing
internal hemorrhage. This torture was called the rack. If
you wanted to burn someone to death without hearing him
scream, you could use a tongue lock, a metal rod between
the jaw and collarbone that prevented him from opening
his mouth. You could put a person in a chair with spikes
on the seat and arms, tie him down against the spikes, and
beat him, so that every time he flinched from the beating
he drove his own flesh deeper onto the spikes. This was the
inquisitor's chair. If you wanted to make it worse, you could
heat the spikes. You could suspend a person over a pointed
wooden pyramid and whenever he started to fall asleep,
you could drop him onto the point. If you were Ippolito
Marsili, the inventor of this torture, known as the Judas
cradle, you could tell yourself you had invented something
humane, a torture that worked without burning flesh or
breaking bones. For the torture here was supposed to be
sleep deprivation.

The secret of torture, like the secret of French cuisine, is that nothing is unthinkable. The human body is like a foodstuff, to be grilled, pounded, filleted. Every opening exists to be stuffed, all flesh to be carved off the bone. You take an ordinary wheel, a heavy wooden wheel with spokes. You lay the victim on the ground with blocks of wood at strategic points under his shoulders, legs, and arms. You use the wheel to break every bone in his body. Next you tie his body onto the wheel. With all its bones broken, it will be pliable. However, the victim will not be dead. If you want to kill him, you hoist the wheel aloft on the end of a pole and leave him to starve. Who would have thought to do this with a man and a wheel? But, then, who would have thought to take the disgusting snail, force it to render its ooze, stuff it in its own shell with garlic butter, bake it, and eat it?

Not long ago I had a facial – only in part because I thought I needed one. It was research into the nature and function of pleasure. In a dark booth at the back of the beauty salon, the aesthetician put me on a table and applied a series of ointments to my face, some cool, some warmed. After a while she put something into my hand, cold and metallic. "Don't be afraid, madame," she said. "It is an electrode. It will not hurt you. The other end is attached to two metal cylinders, which I roll over your face. They break down the electricity barrier on your skin and allow the moisturizers to penetrate deeply." I didn't believe this hocuspocus. I didn't believe in the electricity barrier or in the ability of these rollers to break it down. But it all felt very good. The cold metal on my face was a pleasant change from the soft warmth of the aesthetician's fingers. Still, since Algeria it's hard to hear the word *electrode* without fear. So when she left me for a few minutes with a moist, refreshing cheesecloth over my face, I thought, What if the goal of her expertise were pain, not moisture? What if the electrodes were electrodes in the Algerian sense? What if the cheesecloth mask were dipped in acid?

In Paris, where the body is so pampered, torture seems particularly sinister, not because it's hard to understand but because — as the dark side of sensuality — it seems so easy. Beauty care is among the glories of Paris. *Soins esthétiques* include makeup, facials, massages (both relaxing and reducing), depilations (partial and complete), manicures, pedicures, and tanning, in addition to the usual run of *soins* for the hair: cutting, brushing, setting, waving, styling, blowing, coloring, and streaking. In Paris the state of your skin, hair, and nerves is taken seriously, and there is little of the puritanical thinking that tries to persuade us that beauty comes from within. Nor do the French think, as Americans do, that beauty should be offhand and low-maintenance. Spending time and money on *soins esthéthiques* is appropriate and necessary, not self-indulgent. Should that loving attention to the body turn malevolent, you have torture. You have the procedure — the aesthetic, as it were — of torture, the explanation for the rich diversity of torture instruments, but you do not have the cause.

Historically torture has been a tool of legal systems, used to get information needed for a trial or, more directly, to determine guilt or innocence. In the Middle Ages confession was considered the best of all proofs, and torture was the way to produce a confession, In other words, torture didn't come into existence to give vent to human sadism. It is not always private and perverse but sometimes social and institutional, vetted by the government and, of course, the Church. (There have been few bigger fans of torture than Christianity and Islam.) Righteousness, as much a viciousness, produces torture. There aren't squads of sadists beating down the doors to the torture chambers begging for jobs. Rather, as a recent book on torture by Edward Peters says, the institution of torture creates sadists; the weight of a culture, Peters suggests, is necessary to recruit torturers. You have to convince people that they are working for a great goal in order to get them to overcome their repugnance to the task of causing physical pain to another person. Usually the great goal is the preservation of society, and the victim is presented to the torturer as being in some way out to destroy it.

From another point of view, what's horrifying is how easily you can convince someone that he is working for the common good. Perhaps the most appalling psychological experiment of modern times, by Stanley Milgram, showed that ordinary, decent people in New Haven, Connecticut, could be brought to the point of inflicting (as they thought) severe electric shocks on other people in obedience to an authority and in pursuit of a goal, the advancement of knowledge, of which they approved. Milgram used – some would say abused – the prestige of science and the university to make his point, but his point is chilling nonetheless. We can cluck over torture, but the evidence at least suggests that with intelligent handling most of us could be brought to do it ourselves.

In the Middle Ages, Milgram's experiment would have had no point. It would have shocked no one that people were capable of cruelty in the interest of something they believed in. That was as it should be. Only recently in the history of human thought has the avoidance of cruelty moved to the forefront of ethics. "Putting cruelty first," as Judith Shklar says in *Ordinary Vices*, is comparatively new. The belief that the "pursuit of happiness" is one of man's inalienable rights, the idea that "cruel and unusual punishment" is an evil in itself, the Benthamite notion that behavior should be guided by what will produce the greatest happiness for the greatest number – all these principles are only two centuries old. They were born with the eighteenth-century democratic revolutions. And in two hundred years they have not been universally accepted. Wherever people believe strongly in some cause, they will justify torture – not just the Nazis, but the French in Algeria.

Many people who wouldn't hurt a fly have annexed to fashion the imagery of torture – the thongs and spikes and metal studs – hence reducing it to the frivolous and transitory. Because torture has been in the mainstream and not on the margins of history, nothing could be healthier.

For torture to be merely kinky would be a big advance. Exhibitions like the one I saw in Paris, which presented itself as educational, may be guilty of pandering to the tastes they deplore. Solemnity may be the wrong tone. If taking one's goals too seriously is the danger, the best discouragement of torture may be a radical hedonism that denies that any goal is worth the means, that refuses to allow the nobly abstract to seduce us from the sweetness of the concrete. Give people a good croissant and a good cup of coffee in the morning. Give them an occasional facial and a plate of escargots. Marie Antoinette picked a bad moment to say "Let them eat cake," but I've often thought she was on the right track.

All of which brings me back to Paris, for Paris exists in the imagination of much of the world as the capital of pleasure — of fun, food, art, folly, seduction, gallantry, and beauty. Paris is civilization's reminder to itself that nothing leads you less wrong than your awareness of your own pleasure and a genial desire to spread it around. In that sense the myth of Paris constitutes a moral touchstone, standing for the selfish frivolity that helps keep priorities straight. ✖

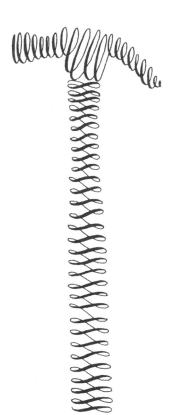

SCOTT RUSSELL SANDERS

The Inheritance of Tools*

AT JUST ABOUT THE HOUR when my father died, soon after dawn one February morning when ice coated the windows like cataracts, I banged my thumb with a hammer. Naturally I swore at the hammer, the reckless thing, and in the moment of swearing I thought of what my father would say: "If you'd try hitting the nail it would go in a whole lot faster. Don't you know your thumb's not as hard as that hammer?" We both were doing carpentry that day, but far apart. He was building cupboards at my brother's place in Oklahoma; I was at home in Indiana putting up a wall in the basement to make a bedroom for my daughter. By the time my mother called with news of his death – the long distance wires whittling her voice until it seemed too thin to bear the weight of what she had to say – my thumb was swollen. A week or so later a white scar in the shape of a crescent moon began to show above the cuticle, and month by month it rose across the pink sky of my thumbnail. It took the better part of a year for the scar to disappear, and every time I noticed it I thought of my father.

---

* From *The Paradise of Bombs* (Beacon Press, 1992).

The hammer had belonged to him, and to his father before him. The three of us have used it to build houses and barns and chicken coops, to upholster chairs and crack walnuts, to make doll furniture and bookshelves and jewelry boxes. The head is scratched and pockmarked, like an old plowshare that has been working rocky fields, and it gives off the sort of dull sheen you see on fast creek water in the shade. It is a finishing hammer, about the weight of a bread loaf, too light really for framing walls, too heavy for cabinetwork, with a curved claw for pulling nails, a rounded head for pounding, a fluted neck for looks, and a hickory handle for strength.

The present handle is my third one, bought from a lumberyard in Tennessee down the road from where my brother and I were helping my father build his retirement house. I broke the previous one by trying to pull sixteen penny nails out of floor joists – a foolish thing to do with a finishing hammer, as my father pointed out. "You ever hear of a crowbar?" he said. No telling how many handles he and my grandfather had gone through before me. My grandfather used to cut down hickory trees on his farm, saw them into slabs, cure the planks in his hayloft, and carve handles with a drawknife. The grain in hickory is crooked and knotty, and therefore tough, hard to split, like the grain in the two men who owned this hammer before me.

After proposing marriage to a neighbor girl, my grandfather used this hammer to build a house for his bride on a stretch of river bottom in northern Mississippi. The lumber for the place, like the hickory for the handle, was cut on his own land. By the day of the wedding he had not quite finished the house, and so right after the ceremony he took his wife home and put her to work. My grandmother had worn her Sunday dress for the wedding, with a fringe of lace tacked on around the hem in honor of the occasion. She removed this lace and folded it away before going out to help my grandfather nail siding on the house. "There she was in her good dress," he told me some fifty-odd years after that wedding day, "holding up them long pieces of clapboard while I hammered, and together we got the place covered up before dark." As the family grew to four, six, eight, and eventually thirteen, my grandfather used this hammer to enlarge his house room by room, like a chambered nautilus expanding his shell.

By and by the hammer was passed along to my father. One day he was up on the roof of our pony barn nailing shingles with it, when I stepped out the kitchen door to call him for supper. Before I could yell, something about the sight of him straddling the spine of that roof and swinging the hammer caught my eye and made me hold my tongue. I was five or six years old, and the world's commonplaces were still news to me. He would pull a nail from the pouch at his waist, bring the hammer down, and a moment later the *thunk* of the blow would reach my ears. And that is what had stopped me in my tracks and stilled my tongue, that momentary gap between seeing and hearing the blow. Instead of yelling from the kitchen door, I ran to the barn and climbed two rungs up the ladder — as far as I was allowed to go – and spoke quietly to my father. On our walk to the house he explained that sound takes time to make its way through air. Suddenly the world seemed larger, the air more dense, if sound could be held back like any ordinary traveler.

By the time I started using this hammer, at about the age when I discovered the speed of sound, it already contained houses and mysteries for me. The smooth handle was one my grandfather had made. In those days I needed both hands to swing it. My father would start a nail in a scrap of wood, and I would pound away until I bent it over.

"Looks like you got ahold of some of those rubber nails," he would tell me. "Here, let me see if I can find you some stiff ones." And he would rummage in a drawer until he came up with a fistful of more cooperative nails. "Look at the head," he would tell me. "Don't look at your hands, don't look at the hammer. Just look at the head of that nail and pretty soon you'll learn to hit it square."

Pretty soon I did learn. While he worked in the garage cutting dovetail joints for a drawer or skinning a deer or tuning an engine, I would hammer nails. I made innocent blocks of wood look like porcupines. He did not talk much in the midst of his tools, but he kept up a nearly ceaseless humming, slipping in and out of a dozen tunes in an afternoon, often running back over the same stretch of melody again and again, as if searching for a way out. When the humming did cease, I knew he was faced with a task requiring great delicacy or concentration, and I took care not to distract him.

He kept scraps of wood in a cardboard box – the ends of two-by-fours, slabs of shelving and plywood, odd pieces of molding – and everything in it was fair game. I nailed scraps together to fashion what I called boats or houses, but the results usually bore only faint resemblance to the visions I carried in my head. I would hold up these constructions to show my father, and he would turn them over in his hands admiringly, speculating about what they might be. My cobbled-together guitars might have been alien spaceships, my barns might have been models of Aztec temples, each wooden contraption might have been anything but what I had set out to make.

Now and again I would feel the need to have a chunk of wood shaped or shortened before I riddled it with nails, and I would clamp it in a vice and scrape at it with a handsaw. My father would let me lacerate the board until my arm gave out, and then he would wrap his hand around mine and help me finish the cut, showing me how to use my thumb to guide the blade, how to pull back on the saw to keep it from binding, how to let my shoulder do the work.

"Don't force it," he would say, "just drag it easy and give the teeth a chance to bite."

As the saw teeth bit down the wood released its smell, each kind with its own fragrance, oak or walnut or cherry or pine, usually pine because it was the softest, easiest for a child to work. No matter how weathered and gray the board, no matter how warped and cracked, inside there was this smell waiting, as of something freshly baked. I gathered every smidgen of sawdust and stored it away in coffee cans, which I kept in a drawer of the workbench. When I did not feel like hammering nails I would dump my sawdust on the concrete floor of the garage and landscape it into highways and farms and towns, running miniature cars and trucks along miniature roads. Looming as huge as a colossus, my father worked over and around me, now and again bending down to inspect my work, careful not to trample my creations. It was a landscape that smelled dizzyingly of wood. Even after a bath my skin would carry the smell, and so would my father's hair, when he lifted me for a bedtime hug.

I tell these things not only from memory but also from recent observation, because my own son now turns blocks of wood into nailed porcupines, dumps cans full of sawdust at my feet and sculpts highways on the floor. He learns how to swing a hammer from the elbow instead of the wrist, how to lay his thumb beside the blade to guide a saw, how to tap a chisel with a wooden mallet, how to mark a hole with an awl before starting a drill bit. My daughter did the same before him, and even now, on the brink of teenage aloofness, she will occasionally drag out my box of wood scraps and carpenter something. So I have seen my apprenticeship to wood and tools reenacted in each of my children, as my father saw his own apprenticeship renewed in me.

The saw I use belonged to him, as did my level and both of my squares, and all four tools had belonged to his father. The blade of the saw is the bluish color of gun barrels, and the maple handle, dark from the sweat of hands, is inscribed with curving leaf designs. The level is a shaft of walnut two feet long, edged with brass and pierced by three round windows in which air bubbles float in oil-filled tubes of glass. The middle window serves for testing if a surface is horizontal, the others for testing if a surface is plumb or vertical. My grandfather used to carry this level on the gun-rack behind the seat in his pickup, and when I rode with him I would turn around to watch the bubbles dance. The larger of the two squares is called a framing square, a flat steel elbow, so beat up and tarnished you can barely make out the rows of numbers that show how to figure the cuts on rafters. The smaller one is called a try square, for marking right angles, with a blued steel blade for the shank and a brass-faced block of cherry for the head.

I was taught early on that a saw is not to be used apart from a square: "If you're going to cut a piece of wood," my father insisted, "you owe it to the tree to cut it straight."

Long before studying geometry, I learned there is a mystical virtue in right angles. There is an unspoken morality in seeking the level and the plumb. A house will stand, a table will bear weight, the sides of a box will hold together only if the joints are square and the members upright. When the bubble is lined up between two marks etched in the glass tube of a level, you have aligned yourself with the forces that hold the universe together. When you miter the corners of a picture frame, each angle must be exactly forty-five degrees, as they are in the perfect triangles of Pythagoras, not a degree more or less. Otherwise the frame will hang crookedly, as if ashamed of itself and of its maker.

No matter if the joints you are cutting do not show. Even if you are butting two pieces of wood together inside a cabinet, where no one except a wrecking crew will ever see them, you must take pains to insure that the ends are square and the studs are plumb.

I took pains over the wall I was building on the day my father died. Not long after that wall was finished-paneled with tongue-and-groove boards of yellow pine, the nail holes filled with putty and the wood all stained and sealed — I came close to wrecking it one afternoon when my daughter ran howling up the stairs to announce that her gerbils had escaped from their cage and were hiding in my brand new wall. She could hear them scratching and squeaking behind her bed. Impossible! I said. How on earth could they get inside my drum-tight wall? Through the heating vent, she answered. I went downstairs, pressed my ear to the honey-colored wood, and heard the scritch scritch of tiny feet.

"What can we do?" my daughter wailed. "They'll starve to death, they'll die of thirst, they'll suffocate."

"Hold on," I soothed. "I'll think of something."

While I thought and she fretted, the radio on her bedside table delivered us the headlines. Several thousand people had died in a city in India from a poisonous cloud that had leaked overnight from a chemical plant. A nuclear-powered submarine had been launched. Rioting continued in South Africa. An airplane had been hijacked in the Mediterranean. Authorities calculated that several thousand homeless people slept on the streets within sight of the Washington Monument. I felt my usual helplessness in face of all these calamities. But here was my daughter weeping because her gerbils were holed up in a wall. This calamity I could handle.

"Don't worry," I told her. "We'll set food and water by the heating vent and lure them out. And if that doesn't do the trick, I'll tear the wall apart until we find them."

She stopped crying and gazed at me. "You'd really tear it apart? Just for my gerbils? The *wall?*" Astonishment slowed her down only for a second, however, before she ran to the workbench and began tugging at drawers, saying, "Let's see, what'll we need? Crowbar. Hammer. Chisels. I hope we don't have to use them-but just in case."

We didn't need the wrecking tools. I never had to assault my handsome wall, because the gerbils eventually came out to nibble at a dish of popcorn. But for several hours I studied the tongue-and-groove skin I had nailed up on the day of my father's death, considering where to begin prying. There were no gaps in that wall, no crooked joints.

I had botched a great many pieces of wood before I mastered the right angle with a saw, botched even more before I learned to miter a joint. The knowledge of these things resides in my hands and eyes and the webwork of muscles, not in the tools. There are machines for sale – powered miter boxes and radial arms saws, for instance – that will enable any casual soul to cut proper angles in boards. The skill is invested in the gadget instead of the person who uses it, and this is what distinguishes a machine from a tool. If I had to earn my keep by making furniture or building houses, I suppose I would buy powered saws and pneumatic nailers; the need for speed would drive me to it. But since I carpenter only for my own pleasure or to help neighbors or to remake the house around the ears of my family, I stick with hand tools. Most of the ones I own were given to me by my father, who also taught me how to wield them. The tools in my workbench are a double inheritance, for each hammer and level and saw is wrapped in a cloud of knowing.

All of these tools are a pleasure to look at and to hold. Merchants would never paste NEW NEW NEW! signs on them in stores. Their designs are old because they work, because they serve their purpose well. Like folksongs and aphorisms and the grainy bits of language, these tools have been pared down to essentials. I look at my claw hammer, the distillation of a hundred generations of carpenters, and consider that it holds up well beside those other classics – Greek vases, Gregorian chants, 'Don Quixote, barbed fish hooks, candles, spoons. Knowledge of hammering stretches back to the earliest humans who squatted beside fires chipping flints. Anthropologists have a lovely name for those unworked rocks that served as the earliest hammers. Dawn stones, they are called. Their only qualification for the work, aside from hardness, is that they fit the hand. Our ancestors used them for grinding corn, tapping awls, smashing bones. From dawn stones to this claw hammer is a great leap in time, but no great distance in design or imagination.

On that iced-over February morning when I smashed my thumb with the hammer, I was down in the basement framing the wall that my daughter's gerbils would later hide in. I was thinking of my father, as I always did whenever I built anything, thinking how he would have gone about the work, hearing in memory what he would have said about the wisdom of hitting the nail instead of my thumb. I had the studs and plates nailed together all square and trim, and was lifting the wall into place when the phone rang upstairs. My wife answered, and in a moment she came to the basement door and called down softly to me. The stillness in her voice made me drop the framed wall and hurry upstairs. She told me my father was dead. Then I heard the details over the phone from my mother. Building a set of cupboards for my brother in Oklahoma, he had knocked off work early the previous afternoon because of cramps in his stomach. Early this morning, on his way into the kitchen of my brother's trailer, maybe going for a glass of water, so early that no one else was awake, he slumped down on the linoleum and his heart quit.

For several hours I paced around inside my house, upstairs and down, in and out of every room, looking for the right door to open and knowing there was no such door. My wife and children followed me and wrapped me in arms and backed away again, circling and staring as if I were on fire. Where was the door, the door, the door? I kept wondering. My smashed thumb turned purple and throbbed, making me furious. I wanted to cut it off and rush outside and scrape away the snow and hack a hole in the frozen earth and bury the shameful thing.

I went down into the basement, opened a drawer in my workbench, and stared at the ranks of chisels and knives.

Oiled and sharp, as my father would have kept them, they gleamed at me like teeth. I took up a clasp knife, pried out the longest blade, and tested the edge on the hair of my forearm. A tuft came away cleanly, and I saw my father testing the sharpness of tools on his own skin, the blades of axes and knives and gouges and hoes, saw the red hair shaved off in patches from his arms and the backs of his hands. "That will cut bear," he would say. He never cut a bear with his blades, now my blades, but he cut deer, dirt, wood. I closed the knife and put it away. Then I took up the hammer and went back to work on my daughter's wall, snugging the bottom plate against a chalkline on the floor, shimming the top plate against the joists overhead, plumbing the studs with my level, making sure before I drove the first nail that every line was square and true. ❧

JENN BRISENDINE

Oh hell! What have we here?

WHILE PURÉEING carrots the other day, I was thinking about Shakespeare's Lady Macbeth. Her deft calculations as she manipulates her husband into murder have always fascinated me, and I was deliberating over a choice of animal symbols for this would-be queen: A snake? A tigress? A shark? No, I decided, scraping out the last of the carrots. Lady Macbeth best embodies the duality of a wolf, smart but sly, making silent and strategic tracks in the cold. Like the most intelligent female in a wolf pack, she sees the opportunity for her mate to rise to alpha male, and drives him to it. The carrots were for the baby; the ponderings on Lady M. were strictly for me.

A bit caught up, I tapped the spoon too hard and drops of puréed carrot rained down on my white shirt. I couldn't help it: "Out, damn spot,"* I said, and my four-year-old giggled. I restrained myself from saying it again, but grinned and made exaggerated hand-wiping gestures under the running water.

---

*   Lady Macbeth, *Macbeth*, Act V Scene i

You'd be amazed at the number of references to the mighty works of Will that come up around here. Suitable lines surface with a curious immediacy: "Come not between the dragon and his wrath,"* I'll warn my husband of the baby in a fussy mood. Or, a personal favorite of mine, "Oh hell! What have we here?"† – a perfect line to use at the discovery of a suddenly-appearing mystery pile of Lumpy Something on the carpet. Is it (A) baby-chewed-and-spewed rug fuzz, (B) an undersized cat hairball, (C) the end result of a dog sneak-and-destroy mission, (D) a rejected mound of preschooler lunch, or (E) none of the above? Is Shakespeare cringing even now under the stones of Holy Trinity Church as I invoke his words at the sight of unidentifiable gray matter?

My appreciation for this playwright runs a lot deeper than these handy, sometimes irreverent line quotations. I'm not a Shakespeare scholar, but I am a front-row student with a big crush on the teacher. My infatuation with Mr. Shakespeare started in high school and has persisted for twenty years. It was love-at-first-read in the 12th grade, thanks to a romanticized absorption of *Macbeth*, *King Lear*, and *Hamlet*. College drama and Brit Lit courses played host to hours of staged Shakespeare in my head. My post-grad-

---

*   Lear, *King Lear*, Act I Scene i

†   Morocco, *The Merchant of Venice*, Act II Scene vii

uate years of acting, directing, and teaching have cemented a centuries-spanning bond between us. I'm no authority, just a buff, a devotee, a not-so-secret admirer.

But buff was good enough for the teachers and students of the high school in which I taught for ten years. By default they turned to me, the Shakespeare Specialist, for resources on the plays, the characters, and the speeches. I led students, some of whom had never before seen a play, up to the auditorium stage to block the stabbing scene in *Caesar*. I quizzed my students: "Who said, 'A plague o' both your houses!'?"* And I helped student actors prepare for the annual Shakespeare monologue contest.

I left teaching, and all that went with it, when I had my second son. Getting myself dressed at 5:00 AM, the daily dose of mouthy and resistant teenagers, the bureaucratic nightmare of standardized testing – I am happy to have left those things behind. But my Shakespeare lessons … oh my. Parting is such … you know.

Now my days are filled with preschool drop-offs and pickups, 3:00 AM feedings (still, at nine months! "Aye, there's the rub."†), starter science experiments, and endless laundry. I am engrossed in the needs of my sons, happier than I have ever been, and full to the brim emotionally, spiritually, maternally.

But mentally … well, there I get by with a little help from my friend. Though my Shakespeare texts have been

---

*   Mercutio, *Romeo and Juliet*, Act III Scene i

†   Hamlet, *Hamlet*, Act III Scene i

relegated to an unreachable shelf in the living room, I still run through entire plotlines in my head. I recall favorite phrases and couplets. I picture a character making a crucial connection, or another whispering a secret aside, and I feel the old thrill.

There's a bit of an isolation factor, you see, with being a stay-at-home, work-from-home parent even in these heady days of instant electronic and virtual gratification. Long hours of age-appropriate activities, a few too many episodes of *Speed Racer*, the colorless deep-freeze of a western Pennsylvania winter of discontent, all of these flood together and become as hopelessly entangled as the spent yo-yos and long-legged gummy bugs in the junk drawer. I no longer recoil at the fearful thought of the gnarled and monstrous Caliban, isolated and confined on his island. In fact, I sympathize with the guy and feel like I should bake him some brownies.

To combat Caliban Syndrome, I let my love of Shakespeare rekindle my brain. Phrases and ideas animate me as if whispered by a prompter in the wings. For example, I have a habit of coining sentences with a nod to the Bard's way with words. I might first mutter to my son, "This room's a wreck, Aidan." But then, inspired by a stroke of Elizabethan genius, I re-craft the sentence: "Zounds, you muffin-straggler! Th' abode afflicts my eyes with pangs of woe." Aidan is not sure why he's been called a muffin-something, but he thinks it's hilarious.

Sometimes, the Elizabethan-style lingo is just mundane commentary: A surprisingly high bill at the grocery store elicits, "Accursed cost of living in this town." That gets the iambic pentameter bonus. Or maybe the words well up while watching the baby sleep: "Scented with love, easy-minded and blessed; nomad wand'ring to dreamful rest."

This verbal hobby is a fun preoccupation for average days. For the not-so-normal, I haul out the big Greek guns: catharsis, or When Someone Else's Day is Way Worse Than Mine, I Feel Better. I keep a mental catalog of plot points for moments when the culminating effect of day-to-day mini-stresses sets my head rolling. Say, for example, that my four-year old has a yelling fit when a toy breaks, which sets off the baby, sure as if you'd poked him with a rapier. The baby's wails bring the puppy running, and in comforting the baby I miss the sniff-and-squat sequence until it's too late. Cleaning up dog pee, I don't hear the timer, so I overcook to a nice broiled sandpaper-texture the cookies for the preschool program. Combine these events with the curt form rejection to the latest novel query, plus the phone message from my husband that tells me his work will keep him on the road for the fifth night this week, and here comes that airless feeling in my chest, like it's filling with frantic bees.

Individually, none of these are fall-on-your-own-sword events, but the cumulative effect requires some kind of coping mechanism. Some caregivers take a step out on the porch. Some just laugh and dig in harder. I compare my own plotline to Juliet's. How the heck must she have felt, waking up in a corpse-filled crypt beneath the warm weight of her dead love, piecing together how miserably her plan has failed? Could it have gone any worse for her? Not much. How much worse could it be for me? Obviously, dog pee and burnt baked goods don't compare to Juliet's fate. Bring on the screaming mee-mees, boys. I'm fine now.

I also love the cathartic effect *Richard II* has on me. Lord, that guy has it bad: so high in position, so low in potential. He is so confident that God has blessed his rule that he thinks his kingship cannot go wrong, when in fact, he's a perfectly lousy king and is about to be overthrown. When he realizes that his defenders have deserted him:

> Let's talk of graves, of worms, and epitaphs,
> Make dust our paper, and with rainy eyes
> Write sorrow on the bosom of the earth.
>
> (King Richard, *Richard II*, Act III Scene ii)

A bad day here? Sure. An awful day? Maybe. But a day so filled with despair that my tears imprint sorrow on the ground? No, surely not. The pathos of another age, another life, resuscitates my spirit.

I use Shakespeare most of all to maintain an inner balance. Shakespeare's wit is most powerful not to contend with others, but to contend with oneself. He nurtures strength and dignity. He instills the confidence, reason, and sense-of-self that are necessary to battle the gnat-like doubts that accompany a switch from contributing breadwinner to primary caretaker.

How exactly does a playwright who died nearly 400 years ago manage to help me here? He's talented, all right, but come on. Helpful in assessing — nay, encouraging — a woman's self-worth? Yea, I say to that. Even as a high school student I lobbied for Shakespeare as an early voice of feminism, a claim by which I stand firm after years of considering the male-female dynamics between his characters. Consider Beatrice's point-for-point banter:

> I had rather hear my dog bark at a crow than a man swear
> he loves me.
> (*Much Ado About Nothing*, Act I Scene i)

or Katharine's risky outspokenness:

> If I be waspish, best beware my sting.
> (*The Taming of the Shrew*, Act II Scene i)

or Cordelia's gentle insistence on the highest truth:

> Unhappy that I am, I cannot heave
> My heart into my mouth: I love your majesty
> According to my bond; nor more nor less.
> (*King Lear*, Act I Scene i)

or Adriana's refusal to forgive her philandering husband:

> Why should their liberty than ours be more?
> (*The Comedy of Errors*, Act II, Scene i)

or Portia's logic and self-assurance:

… I am half yourself,
And I must freely have the half of anything
That this same paper brings you.
                    (*The Merchant of Venice*, Act III, Scene ii)

Shakespeare's females exude strength of character. They are strong-willed, but know when to change their minds. They speak bluntly but demonstrate grace and class. I see facets of them in my mother, my cousins, my aunts, and my friends. Shakespeare's ladies span the gamut of human motivation, from those who are self-serving (Regan and Goneril, against their own father King Lear) to the ones who are wholly dedicated to someone else (loyal Emilia to the doomed Desdemona) to those whose motivations might be a little, well, complicated (my dear Lady M.). The women make decisions and take actions that change the events and directly turn the outcome of the plays. My observations of these female characters' strength metamorphosed into drawing from it. It used to be easy to count my accomplishments (closing night of a production, last day of another school year) and track my contributions to marriage and family (monthly paychecks, dental and vision). Since I quit my job to stay home, it has been far more difficult to assess the value of my work. But consider Rosalind, mistress of disguise in *As You Like It*. She shows me how to change roles on the fly. Hero, the demure and honorable young lady in *Much Ado About Nothing*, proves that time will reveal one's significant deeds. Even Lady Macbeth has lessons for me: on partnership, on gender roles, on ambition. These ladies share generously with me their talents and charms, their warmth and passion, their dangerous and darker sides, and most of all their ability to remain true to their very characters.

While thinking about these Elizabethan ladies, I remembered my Shakespeare books on the top shelf: character dictionaries, anthologies of the plays, prose retellings, Bloom's *Shakespeare: The Invention of the Human*. On a whim, or maybe not, I stood on a chair to reach a picture-book-style text which retells the possible folktale sources of plays like *Hamlet* and *The Merchant of Venice* – dreamy images of peasantry and pageantry splashed across pages in shades reminiscent of Monet's *Water Lilies*. I called to Aidan. He was hooked by the illustration on the book's cover: a youthful Will, reading a book.

"This was a writer who lived a long time ago," I explained, "and he made up plays from the stories he read. His name was William Shakespeare."

"Shakespeare?" Aidan said, tasting the name for the first time.

We read the story about a quarrelsome young woman who learns to value a kind word, an old legend with parallels to *The Taming of the Shrew*. Once finished, Aidan asked me to read another. This four-year-old's instant attachment is proof of Shakespeare's universal appeal. He wrote for everyone, from the nobles on the third tier of the Globe to the nut-eaters in the pit. I am indebted to Shakespeare, in every role I have played – student, teacher, actor, director, wife, parent – precisely because his is a literature of life, alive on the page, breathing on stage, and accessible in everyone's every day. In response to my son I nodded and turned to the next title. "Let us from point to point this story know."* ❧

---

*   King of France, *All's Well That Ends Well*, Act V Scene iii

E. B. WHITE

My Day*

With Mrs. Roosevelt's permission, I shall describe my day. I woke at six and lay till quarter past, slowly turning my head from side to side to test out my neck, which has less play in it than it once had. Was disappointed in my neck but pleased at being able to recall with great clearness a dream I had had in the night. I dreamed that I was in a resort hotel, having dinner, and the manager came over to the table and tapped me peremptorily on the shoulder and said: "Mr. White, you go to your room immediately and take off that old blue sweater and put on your jacket." And straightway I arose and left the room behind the manager, clowning as I went.

So I told the dream to my wife and offered to let her interpret it, which she did. She said it was a perfectly simple dream and merely meant that the manager was probably right. But I think there is more to it than that, and I felt grieved that my wife should have sided with someone I had met in my sleep.

I got out of bed at half-past six, thinking about dreams and about what a plowman had told me the other day –

---

* From *One Man's Meat* (Harper & Bros., 1944).

which was that he often gets the answer to his problems in dreams. He had a dream lately telling him what to do about my newly-laid-down field, where I didn't get a very good catch of grass. He and I were discussing it the other afternoon at quitting time, and he told me next day that he had gone to bed thinking about it and that the answer had come to him as easy as anything.

"What did your dream say we should do?" I asked.

"Put the phosphate to it," he replied cheerfully. A good dream, and sound soil practice, but I wish people would have hallucinations that don't cost me money.

Dressed without shaving, and splashed a cupful of cold water over my face and felt as ready for the day as Jeeter Lester. So down the back stairs noisily and out through the dewy field with Fred, my chore dog, to the chicken range, where I opened the doors of the shelters and watched my two hundred pullets, long pent up, come sailing through the openings like chaff on the wind – a black cloud of feathers and delight. Some of them sprayed themselves out over the green grass, looking for employment; others gathered eagerly at my feet, looking for grain.

On the way back to the house along the hard-packed path, I noticed that a pall of smoke, presumably from forest fires to the north of us, overhung the world; it gave the sky a queer look, a sort of diffused brilliance. All common objects appeared unusual. I was surprised to note, during the course of the day, how many people remarked that it looked "like the end of the world." Why do you suppose people have decided that the end of the world will be pre-

saged by a strange light in the sky? Certainly nobody has
witnessed the event, yet all are agreed that a light will be
noticed in the heavens, perhaps several hours before the
crash. I have a wholly different picture of doomsday – or
rather doomsmoment. I think when the end of the world
comes the sky will be its old blue self, with white cumulus
clouds drifting along. You will be looking out of a window,
say, at a tree; and then after a bit the tree won't be there
any more, and the looking won't be there any more, only
the window will be there, in memory – the thing through
which the looking has been done. I can see God, walking
through the garden and noticing that the world is done for,
reach down and pick it up and put it on His compost pile.
It ought to make a fine ferment.

The plowman mentioned the smoke pall when I was
talking with him in the afternoon, and I asked if he knew
where the fire was.

"Canada," he replied.

"What part of Canada?" I asked.

"The whole of it," he said. "They tell me the whole of
Canada is ablaze."

"That's a big fire then," I answered. "Canada is a large
place, larger than the United States even."

The plowman considered this distasteful pronouncement a moment. "Well then," he said, "it is a big fire." But
he added cheerfully, "Anyways, it'll have to cross a pile of
water 'fore it gits to us."

I nodded in perfect agreement, for this seemed a spiri-
tual rather than a geographical discussion, and I felt in-

structed and renewed. After breakfast I went to the barn with my boy to tend a lamb that had been cut, and while the boy held the lamb I ran some pine tar into the wound to keep the flies away, and then we released it, with its mother and its sister, and the three of them raced down the lane, glad to be back to pasture again after hospitalization. So indoors and settled down to work, and worked diligently for about four minutes and then remembered that I was to call for some children, this being the last day of school and a picnic having been arranged. So into the village in the truck, after wiring the tailboard up with a piece of haywire, to prevent wholesale loss of life. The fourth, fifth, and sixth graders were gathered in the schoolyard with their teacher, who had on trousers in honor of the event, and I wished that I could see again (and in trousers) some of the teachers I had had in grammar school – Miss Hackett and Miss Kirby and Miss Crosby and Miss Douglas and Miss Ihlefeldt and Mrs. Schuyler and Miss Abigail A. Bourne and Miss Sheridan. I remembered with regret that none of them had taken me on a picnic during the eight years I spent with them, and that I had never seen any of them in trousers, and I felt cheated. Loaded the children into the truck and carried them a couple of miles to the shore, where they deployed with hot dogs and began falling into mire pots, and left them there and went back to work. Worked for ten or fifteen minutes, but remembered that I had agreed to fetch a roll here, for rolling my field, and that it was about four miles away in the barn of the old Herrick place and that it was probably as big as a house.

I got a fellow to go along with me, and we took a chain, a bar, an ax, a tackle, a few lengths of rope, and some plank, and set off, I being glad, as always, to be self-released from indoor work and glad to be visiting the old Herrick place, which is remote and quiet – an old tumbledown barn in a run-out field encircled by woods and overlooking a small secluded cove. Lilacs were in bloom by the old cellar hole, and a few old apple trees stood guard over the secrets of other days. The world stood still here in this peaceful and mysterious place, which seemed perfect for a tryst or a double suicide. The barn floor was matted with ancient hay, and there was a tedder stored in one corner, and the roll in another, and a few old magazines and junk of one sort or another. As we lifted the tongue of the roll and stirred the thing, a mouse leaped up and ran the length of it, like a tiny dog performing a circus act. I thought how pleasant it would be to start life fresh on the old Herrick place, with a one-room shack and no appurtenances – no equipment, no stock, no pets, no family responsibilities, no program. But knowing myself as well as I do, I well knew that it wouldn't be twenty minutes before I would acquire or con-trive something to establish the roots of complexity in firm soil – a cold chisel perhaps, or an inamorata, or a folding towel rack In no time at all I would destroy the old Herrick place by setting out a pansy plant or repairing a rotten sill. And then it would be just like any other spot – beloved but not removed. A man sometimes gets homesick for the loneliness that he has at one time or another experienced in his life and that is a part of all life in some degree, and sometimes a secluded and half-mournful yet beautiful place will suddenly revive the sensation of pain and melancholy and unfulfillment that are associated with that loneliness, and will make him want to seize it and recapture it; but I know with me it is a passing want and not to be compared with my taste for domesticity, which is most of the time so strong as to be overpowering.

The roll was a big old thing. It was, as I had suspected, made in one long cylinder – narrow ten-foot spruce planks bolted to a pair of old mowing-machine wheels, and the frame heavily constructed. It was as much as the two of us could do to haul it out of its corner, swing it, and start it toward the truck, which I had backed up in the doorway. We made an inclined runway of planks, hooked the tackle on, rigged a snub-line on behind to hold back when we got over the crest, and gave it the works. All went smoothly, the roll crept up the ramp, and we soon had it aboard and lashed down. But our success was of short duration. I started the truck and hadn't gone ten feet when I brought up, all standing, on a rock that was invisible from the driver's seat, and we were hung up for fair, with our load aboard and our right running board aground.

"I guess we got some trouble now," said the fellow that was with me.

We got out the jack, a pitiful little hydraulic affair painted a bright yellow to make it seem alert. Like most jacks, this one had a hernia, and wasn't supposed to lift anything. I got some junks of plank and some short boards, and we spent a happy morning jacking and (as Father Divine would say) rejacking. The jack gave us only a two-inch gain each time, and we would have to catch this gain by trigging up the wheel with wedges. Then we'd take a new footing for our jack and grab another inch or two. But it was nice there, lying full length in the tall sweet grass, and neither of us wanted to be any place else particularly. And finally we cleared the rock and backed off and squared away for home, with our wide enormous cargo.

Found the mail waiting when I got back to the house, and among other items a notice from the secretary of the class of 1921, advising me that it has been twenty years since I graduated. "Get together a gang and come to Ithaca," the announcement said. "See your friends." Then followed a list of their names, and I studied it a long time in vain.

I suppose a man ought to get back to reunion in one of the few remaining Junes of his life, but I never seem to get round to it. I keep saying to myself, "Well, you've just recently graduated, why don't you wait a little spell?" It seems nonsensical to me that I am twenty years gone. When I was an undergraduate and met an alumnus twenty years out, I regarded him as shrivelled beyond repair. Just hulks of men, these old fellows seemed to me – dry stalks, autumnal creatures, about to die.

I have decided not to go back this year, and I guess the thing that decided me was the casual reference in the letter to "the costume." That was the crowning deterrent. I might be able to undergo the embarrassment of saluting dim forgotten classmates with the wrong nicknames, and having my hand pumped by familiar-looking strangers, but I doubted that I could go through with "the costume." A costume would simply make me drink a great deal, very fast, and I can achieve that sort of delirium right here in my own cool cellar. Besides, it gave me considerable pause to realize that sartorially I have slipped like the devil since 1921 and that my everyday garb might easily be construed as a "costume" by other members of my class.

Another piece of mail was a communication from my county agent, Mr. Tibbetts. He reports rainfall below normal, which is an understatement: the ground is powdery, and some wells around here are dry for the first time in years. And he recommends that old hens be kept through the summer, which I intend to do; but I would like to get mine outdoors on green grass if I can, as they are at loose ends nowadays in their pen in the barn. In winter the pen is warm and snug, but in summer it is dusty and dull. Hens need excitement to keep them at peak production. Any little trinket that you bring a hen stimulates her, whether it is the claw of a lobster or a jade bracelet.

We had stewed rhubarb for lunch. It was from stewed rhubarb that the gods got their idea for ambrosia. This year we're going to try putting up rhubarb, which I am told is simple – just cold water, no processing. After lunch studied, in the *Mercury*, Bertrand Russell's blueprint for an enduring peace. He advocates an alliance or league. The weakness of this sort of structure of course is that the whole thing hangs on an agreement, and there is nothing more likely to start disagreement among people or countries than an agreement. I had rather see an attempt at union than an attempt at an alliance, for then the participants would be bound in fact rather than in words. A marriage of convenience between two great democracies is a conceivable thing, but it mustn't be companionate, it must be the real article. But I agree with Dr. Russell that before we can have any sort of peace, enduring or ephemeral, Hitler must be defeated, and I don't think we can accomplish that by blacking out Newark, NJ.

In the afternoon drove to the hospital for an injection, taking the laundry with me to be dropped off on the way. In town purchased ten feet of half-inch pipe and stopped in for a while to visit with a man who is building a boat, and was pleased to observe that, like myself, he was glad of any interruption from work, no matter of what nature. Home and found two female artists, so mixed a drink and they stayed for supper, of meatballs, which we apologized for but which they gobbled hungrily, it seemed to me, and gratefully. Listened to Elmer Davis at 8:55 and then out to the barn to put things to bed. In the hen pen searched the nests for broodies, and found one, and removed her, she lying quietly in my arms in the twilight with that wonderful concentrated quietude the fever of incubation induces. The smoke pall of morning had cleared away and the night was sweet and clear, with a heavy integument of lilac. In the brooder house the young cockerels were assembling in a corner, so I took a bamboo pole and rattled it and they quickly found the roosts. Then I closed the pophole. I filled a bucket with oats and continued on to the range where the pullets are, the air here smelling of blossoms with a trace of skunk, and I filled the inside feeders with oats against the morning and closed the doors of the shelters and watched the pullets settling down rank after rank with the tiny burbling sighs of contentment while the mosquitoes tore at me and the warmth and smell rose to greet me from the relaxed bodies of the birds; and I returned to the house and got the terrier and put him in the garage and then let the big red dachshund out and then in again and then the little black dachshund out and in again and I set up the fire screen in the living room and closed the door of the woodshed and turned out the lights one by one through all the rooms and ascended and brushed my teeth and pulled the window curtains and looked in at the sleeping boy to see if he was covered, and undressed and got into bed and tried my neck again and changed position from the right side to the left side and heaved a great long sigh and that (to quote Mr. Davis) is the news to this moment. ❧

CHRISTOPHER MORLEY

Safety Pins*

*L*IGATURE OF INFANCY, healing engine of emergency, base and mainstay of our civilization – we celebrate the safety pin.

What would we do without safety pins? Is it not odd to think, looking about us on our fellowmen (bearded realtors, ejaculating poets, plump and ruddy policemen, even the cheerful man who runs the elevator and whistles "Oh, What a Pal Was Mary" as the clock draws near 6 PM) – all these were first housed and swaddled and made seemly with a paper of safety pins. How is it that the inventor who first conferred this great gift on the world is not known by name for the admiration and applause of posterity? Was it not the safety pin that made the world safe for infancy?

There will be some, mayhap, to set up the button as rival to the safety pin in service to humanity. But our homage bends toward the former. Not only was it our shield and buckler when we were too puny and impish to help ourselves, but it is also (now we are parent) symbol of many a hard-fought field, where we have campaigned all over the

---

*   From *Pipefuls* (Doubleday, Page & Co., 1920).

white counterpane of a large bed to establish an urchin in his proper gear, while he kicked and scrambled, witless of our dismay. It is fortunate, pardee, that human memory does not extend backward to the safety pin era – happily the recording carbon sheet of the mind is not inserted on the roller of experience until after the singular humiliations of earliest childhood have passed. Otherwise our first recollection would doubtless be of the grimly flushed large face of a resolute parent, bending hotly downward in effort to make both ends meet while we wambled and waggled in innocent, maddening sport. In those days when life was (as George Herbert puts it) "assorted sorrows, anguish of all sizes," the safety pin was the only thing that raised us above the bandar-log. No wonder the antique schoolmen used to enjoy computing the number of angels that might dance on the point of a pin. But only archangels would be worthy to pirouette on a safety pin, which is indeed mightier than the sword. When Adam delved and Eve did spin, what did they do for a safety pin?

Great is the stride when an infant passes from the safety pin period to the age of buttons. There are three ages of human beings in this matter: (1) Safety pins, (2) Buttons, (3) Studs, or (for females) Hooks and Eyes. Now there is an interim in the life of man when he passes away from safety pins, and, for a season, knows them not – save as mere convenience in case of breakdown. He thinks of them, in his antic bachelor years, as merely the wrecking train of the sartorial system, a casual conjunction for pyjamas, or an impromptu hoist for small clothes. Ah! with humility and gratitude he greets them again later, seeing them at their true worth, the symbol of integration for the whole social fabric. Women, with their intuitive wisdom, are more subtle in this subject. They never wholly outgrow safety pins, and though they love to ornament them with jewellery, precious metal, and enamels, they are naught but safety pins after all. Some ingenious philosopher could write a full tractate on woman in her relation to pins – hairpins, clothes pins, rolling pins, hatpins.

Only a bachelor, as we have implied, scoffs at pins. Hamlet remarked, after seeing the ghost, and not having any Sir Oliver Lodge handy to reassure him, that he did not value his life at a pin's fee. Pope, we believe, coined the contemptuous phrase, "I care not a pin." The pin has never been done justice in the world of poetry. As one might say, the pin has had no Pindar. Of course there is the old saw about see a pin and pick it up, all the day you'll have good luck. This couplet, barbarous as it is in its false rhyme, points (as Mother Goose generally does) to a profound truth. When you see a pin, you must pick it up. In other words, it is on the floor, where pins generally are. Their instinctive affinity for terra firma makes one wonder why they, rather than the apple, did not suggest the law of gravitation to someone long before Newton.

Incidentally, of course, the reason why Adam and Eve were forbidden to pick the apple was that it was supposed to stay on the tree until it fell, and Adam would then have had the credit of spotting the principle of gravitation.

Much more might be said about pins, touching upon

their curious capacity for disappearing, superstitions con-
cerning them, usefulness of hatpins or hairpins as pipe-
cleaners, usefulness of pins to schoolboys, both when bent
for fishing and when filed to an extra point for use on the
boy in the seat in front (honoring him in the breech, as
Hamlet would have said) and their curious habits of turning up in unexpected places, undoubtedly caught by pins
in their long association with the lovelier sex. But of these
useful hyphens of raiment we will merely conclude by saying that those interested in the pin industry will probably
emigrate to England, for we learn from the *Encyclopedia
Britannica* that in that happy island pins are cleaned by
being boiled in weak beer. Let it not be forgotten, however,
that of all kinds, the safety is the King Pin. ❧

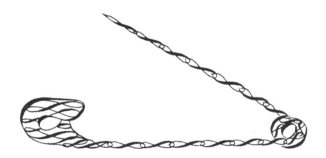

IAN FRAZIER

Bags in Trees*

BAGS IN TREES
(1993)

THIS IS THE SEASON of plastic bags stuck in trees. Stray shopping bags – many of them white, with handles, perhaps from a deli or a fruit-and-vegetable store originally – roll along the streets, fill with air, levitate like disembodied undershirts, fly, snag by their handles in the branches. Trees wave them in the breeze. They luff and whirr like spinnakers and twist into knots. Daniel, a guy who works at the Brooklyn Botanic Garden, was removing a plastic bag from a Japanese flowering cherry tree at the Eastern Parkway entrance with a leaf rake as I walked by. He held the rake above him at arm's length and snatched at the bag with the tines. It took him a while; finally, he pulled the bag down and squashed it into a ball in his hand. I asked if I could see it. Its blue logo read, "MARTIN PAINT ...'It Ain't Just Paint.'"

I walked around Brooklyn looking at plastic bags stuck

---

* A series of three essays, written over a decade, in *Gone to New York: adventures in the city* (Farrar, Straus and Giroux, 2005).

in trees. I got a sore neck from craning up. I saw yellow Tower Records bags, tan bags, red bags like the kind you get in Chinatown, Key Food bags, C-Town bags. Last season's bags have shredded into a sort of plastic Spanish moss. Big black trash bags become involved in branches in a sprawling and complicated way. Over time, light-colored bags darken and dark ones fade until all are a variety of gray. There is a lot of other stuff in trees, too. Second most common, apparently, is audiocassette tape. It wraps around branches and glistens. Next come balloons, both rubber and silvery-plastic. Next come promotional pennants, the kind used-car lots fly. I also saw:

a catalog from a discount office-supply store in a cypress on Washington Avenue

a jacket with a quilted orange lining, a shredded T-shirt, some string, a wad of newspaper, and a red plastic plant hanger in a pin oak at Sixteenth and Prospect Park West

a white baby bunting with a blue-and-pink design and a drawstring at the bottom hem in a tree on Prospect Park West

a white sash, perhaps from a jujitsu uniform, in a tree on McDonald Avenue (there's a jujitsu place just up the street)

a small black folded umbrella in a tree at Fort Hamilton Parkway and Fifty-sixth Street an old tire tied to a tree by a blue fitted sheet printed with Disney characters at the corner of Sixty-first Street

a whitewall bicycle tire in a maple at Seventy-first Street

a piece of angle iron, possibly from a bed frame, in an ailanthus by the highway bridge at Seventy-ninth and Seventh a pair of white Nike high-top sneakers and a pair of high-tops with no visible brand hanging by the laces from a tree at Fifty-ninth Street

thirty-eight pairs of sneakers and other footwear (motorcycle boots, work boots), a pair of dark-red boxing gloves, and a little red-devil doll hanging in a tree at Forty-fifth and Fifth

sneakers, toy guns, teddy bears, and a pair of women's white high-heeled shoes in a big London plane tree on Fifth between Forty-third and Forty-second

a stuffed toy bunny, more women's shoes, more sneakers, a ball of kite string, and a dish drainer in a London plane tree next to that

in a maple above the Prospect Expressway, an unidentifiable wad of leaves and cotton or wool – possibly a nest.

BAGS IN TREES II
(1994)

LAST YEAR at this time I talked about the phenomenon of plastic bags stuck in trees. I did not mention one fact: I don't like plastic bags stuck in trees. Maybe it was a mistake to notice them in the first place; now I notice them everywhere. The London plane trees on my street in Brooklyn are old for city trees and have grown toward the light and away from the buildings, so that now they lean over the street and nearly meet. In a high branch just across from my window, a cluster of plastic party balloons and ribbons on a stick became lodged in the late 1980s. I watched it go from sort of festive to unrecognizable as it persisted like a debt. Storms that strewed branches all over the street did not budge it. One day, I told my friend Tim about it, and we considered what to do.

At Space Surplus Metals, on Church Street, downtown we bought one eight-and-a-half-foot and one seven-foot length of stout aluminum tube about an inch across. One length of tube just fit inside the other. Tim is a jeweler, and he took both tubes to his shop and drilled holes in them so they could be held together by a bolt and nut, and he made a device to fit into the other end of the narrower length. This device was a configuration of short, bendable steel rods soldered to a piece of brass pipe. It looked, very roughly, like a hand with crooked and spread fingers, the middle finger longer, upright, and sharpened into a cutting hook. Assembled, the snagger (as we called it) was about sixteen feet long. Tim brought it to my house early one morning, and we put it together. It lacked about two feet of reaching the party balloons. I went back inside and got a kitchen stool. Tim is tall, and he stood on the stool on tiptoe. The hook end of the snagger made contact. A few twists, a few pulls, and the ancient remnants fell to the sidewalk. The tree seemed to shiver like an unsaddled horse.

We walked all over my neighborhood plucking bags. The snagger worked great — a twist of the crooked metal fingers would inveigle the bag, then the sharpened hook would cut it free. In just a few hours, we had removed scores of bags. Old, shredded ones took a lot of monkeying around with, but new, fresh ones sometimes came free in a single motion. The sensation was like having your arm suddenly extended sixteen feet, and the satisfaction like getting something out of your eye. Dangling above traffic makes the bags sooty, and they soon turned our hands a graphite color. A woman passed by, looked at us, and said, "Oh, it's the bag-removal guys." Then she asked us to go to her house and remove some bags from the trees in front. She carefully gave us her address. After she walked on, Tim said, "She doesn't know there *are* no bag-removal guys."

Recently, Tim made another length for the snagger. Now we can insinuate it more than twenty-five feet through the airy upper realms of ginkgos and lindens and oaks to snatch bags that had eluded us before and had assumed that they had tenure. Last weekend, we were snagging at Collect Pond Park, a bestrewn square plot of pavement and scuffed dirt and benches surrounded by court buildings downtown. Tim's brother, Bill, came, too, and we spelled each other. Holding your arms up that long is tiring. Tim climbed on a "Don't Walk" sign to reach a very high pink plastic bag. We also removed a leather belt, a pair of sneakers, an electrical cord and plug, and some tulle. We spent an hour on a bunch of unidentifiable plastic – a drop cloth, maybe – draping the branches like an exploded fright wig. People stared at us in uneasy incomprehension. The next day, there were nine new bags in two of the trees we had cleaned.

In the Ohio town where I grew up, only the water tower and the church steeples were higher than the trees. Trees occupied the region between us and the sky, and we spent a lot of time looking up into them to see how strong the wind was, or daydreaming. Plastic bags did not get stuck in them, but I did. Once, I climbed an elm in our backyard and wedged my leg between the trunk and a nearly parallel branch. I could not get my arms around the tree to hold on, and so dangled by my leg and yelled. My mother ran to the house being built across the street, and workmen came with a long two-by-four and pried me free.

BAGS IN TREES: A RETROSPECTIVE
(2004)

FOR MORE THAN ten years now, I've been tangled up with the problem of plastic bags stuck in trees. If I've learned anything from the experience, it's "Be careful what you notice." I was living in Brooklyn; I noticed the many plastic bags flapping by their handles from the high branches of trees, cheerful and confident and out of reach. Noticing led to pondering, pondering led to an invention: the bag snagger, a prong-and-hook device that, when attached to a long pole, removes bags and other debris from trees with satisfying efficiency. My friend Tim McClelland made the first working model in his jewelry studio on Broome Street, downtown. Possessing the tool, we of course had to use it; we immediately set off on a sort of harvest festival of bag snagging.

Tim's older brother, Bill, came, too. With snagger and poles (interlocking ones, of aluminum, at first) stowed in Bill's Taurus, we snagged in every New York borough, sometimes going out twice a week. We found bags everywhere, by the thousand; the ultra fine traffic soot that collects on them covered our hands like graphite. Then our ambition led us farther, on bag-snagging jaunts to Massachusetts, Rhode Island, and New Jersey. From someone at a party I heard that trees along the Mississippi River were full of debris after the big floods of 1993, so one August we drove to the river and did a lot of snagging on both the Illinois and the Missouri sides. An environmental group invited us to come to Los Angeles and help with a cleanup along the Los Angeles River, so Bill and I flew out and snagged bags and debris from the prickly desert flora there. For a long while, bag snagging became our main outdoor recreation, completely obliterating the occasional mornings we'd formerly given to golf.

Bill and Tim and I are all transplanted Midwesterners. They grew up in Michigan, I in Ohio. Bill went to my high school in Ohio. We used to do some wild things. Get Tim to tell you about the time at his parents' house outside Rochester, Michigan, on New Year's Eve when he and I decided it would be a great idea to shoot a flashlight out of a tree from a moving toboggan. We tied the flashlight to a branch above a toboggan run on their property, and we were sitting on the toboggan, Tim in front, me in back, me with a loaded shotgun, both of us scooching with our heels to get the toboggan started, when Bill and his (now) wife, Jean, intervened.

Or another time, this one in my loft in lower Manhattan: Tim and I were sitting around drinking Jack Daniel's and beer, and we took my twenty-gauge shotgun down and started fooling with it. Tim asked if I had any ammo for it, and I said I did, and I went and got it. He asked how you loaded it, and I chambered a shell. It happened that my girlfriend (now wife) had moved out a few weeks earlier. Not long before she left, she had persuaded me, at the cost of much labor and hauling by ropes up the elevator shaft, to add a heavy oak bookshelf to our few loft furnishings. I had never figured out where to put the bookshelf, and it still stood in the middle of the floor at one end of the loft, about forty feet from where Tim and I were sitting. The bookshelf had a back of particle board. Hefting the gun, I looked at the shelf for a while, and listened to determine if my neighbors upstairs and down were home; the floor and ceiling in that loft were thin enough so that I could usually hear my neighbors moving around. Nobody home, I decided. I stood, aimed at the bookshelf, and fired. The sound of a shotgun in a brick-walled, enclosed space like that is indescribably loud. There was also the skittery sound of the birdshot pellets going across the floor on the other side of the big hole they blew in the particle board. I don't think Tim or I had ever laughed that hard.

Blue gun smoke filled the room. I gave the gun to Tim, and he aimed and pulled the trigger. We laughed even harder at this explosion, because now we knew better what to expect. I took the gun and fired again. A thick fog of gun smoke hung everywhere. Just then the buzzer rang. It was Bill and two friends. They came in, saw the gun smoke, saw the empty bottle and beer cans on the floor, saw the spent shells, and heard us babbling. They began to back out the door. Amazingly, though, we were able to persuade them that taking a shot would be really fun, and eventually all three of them (one a pacifist woman nurse) did.

Maybe because we grew up surrounded by space and horizons and long views, we Midwesterners felt confined in the city, or constrained. Sometimes we talked about how cool it would be to see a cargo plane at ten thousand feet drop dozens of yellow Checker cabs over an empty area like the Sheep Meadow in Central Park, and how the taxis would look falling into the city against the blue of the sky; or how cool it would be to get a bucket of golf balls and hit them, one after the next, up Fifth Avenue some deserted Sunday morning. That last fantasy we partially enacted, buying range balls by the gross and hitting them into the East and Hudson rivers from the lower Manhattan shoreline. Stroking a long, soaring drive and bouncing it off a support beam of the Manhattan Bridge gave a deeply pleasurable sensation that began in the shoulders and spread down the spine to the toes.

For us, bag snagging represented a more socialized form of the fun we'd been having, or imagining, before. Snagging gave the thrill of vandalism yet was its opposite – mischievous good, rather than mischievous bad. During our bag-snagging foray along the Mississippi, a woman photographer who accompanied us (I was writing about the adventure for *Outside* magazine) looked at us in puzzlement, trying to get a grasp on our hard-to-explain hobby. Then she asked, "Is this bag snagging part of a twelve-step program, or something, that you guys are involved in?" The question made us stop for a moment. She wasn't right, yet her intuition hadn't been entirely wrong.

It goes without saying that the city was different then. Lower Manhattan, with its tendency to depopulate on weekends, was our favorite bagging ground; we used to take stuff out of trees in public spaces that are closely patrolled or completely fenced off (or nonexistent) now. We even had our own traffic cone, with which we redirected traffic when we wanted to work on a branch overhanging the street. Once or twice, we walked unauthorized and unescorted through private buildings to get to a high entanglement that could be reached only from an inner courtyard. People assumed we had some kind of official status, when in fact we had no status at all.

Only once were we seriously challenged. Tim and I had spent a Saturday afternoon among the London plane trees in the lawn around City Hall, experimenting with the aluminum poles at the greatest extension we had yet tried, forty-five or fifty feet. At that length, the pole tends to bend not just over but back again, in a noodly sine curve that makes it difficult to control. As we were trying to master it, a white Parks Department pickup jerked to a stop on a nearby piece of pavement, and a fierce, burly Parks Department guy named Dave Miller hopped out. He asked us what we were doing, and when we tried to explain cut us off with the information that we were breaking the law and that if we injured the trees we could be fined or jailed.

Again we explained, and a grudging curiosity got the

better of him. High in one of the plane trees nearby, beyond
the reach of anything but a cherry picker, a large plastic
drop cloth had wrapped itself around a crotch of boughs.
Rashly, we offered to take it out while he observed. We
had never before snagged anything that high. Dave Miller
hesitated, then gave his permission and stood back, arms
folded, a scowl on his heavy brow. Tim tried for a while
and budged the drop cloth without freeing it. My heart
was pounding as if we were auditioning on Broadway. As
I watched, I realized that the plastic was in a simple knot
that it could be backed out of. I took over, put the wobbly
pole on the target, pushed and turned the plastic, unknot-
ted it from the tree crotch, and lowered it to the lawn on
the end of the pole like a captured standard. Dave Miller all
but leaped for joy. He had a passerby photograph him with
us, the pole, and the drop cloth, he shook our hands twice,
and on the spot he issued us official Parks Department
volunteer cards.

Eventually, we removed drop cloths by the dozen. In
Manhattan, they are a common kind of high-branch entanglement. They fall into trees from skyscrapers under
construction and other upper-story sites. Tarps, also – you
get a lot of them, especially around bridges. From two trees
under the Williamsburg Bridge, Bill and Tim removed
an immense blue canvas tarp complete with grommets.
Evidently it had blown off the back of a truck and landed
on the trees, smothering and oppressing them like an incu-
bus. In fact, a lot of what ends up in Manhattan's trees falls
into them or is thrown. People get mad and chuck other

people's stuff out the window. Sometimes as we removed a series of objects – Walkman, T-shirt, sneakers, underpants, pajama bottoms – we understood that they had all once been the possessions of the same unfortunate guy.

Of course, the basic thing that gets in a New York City tree is the white plastic deli bag. It reaches the tree with the aid of the wind, or (as I sometimes think) by its own power. With its filmy whiteness and its two looped handles, it suggests a self-levitating undershirt; we have named it the undershirt bag. It does not have a soul, but it imitates one, rising and floating on the exhalations of a subway grate like the disembodied spirits that poets used to converse with in Hell. Its prehensile handles cling to any branch that comes within range, and then grab hold for eternity. This bag is not hard to get out of a tree when it's still fresh, but as it ages and shreds it becomes more difficult. The plastic dry-cleaning bag is its sinister companion. After only a day or two of windshredding, the micron-thick plastic of a dry-cleaning bag is all but unremovable. Almost as common as either of those are audiotape and videotape. We have removed furlongs of both, and Bill (who's a composer) has carefully spliced some of the fragments piece to piece; the result, when played, resembles a door suddenly opened on a hall of howling, tedious demons.

If you spend a lot of time taking bags out of trees, you learn that they don't wish anybody well. It's no accident that a visual convention for spookiness is dangling spiderwebs, moss-draped branches, jungly, heart-of-darkness drooping vines. Though not the Dark Power itself, bags in trees nonetheless act as its minions; or, to put it another way, nothing makes a neighborhood look scarier than barebranch trees draped with plastic-bag shreds above a razorwire fence similarly fluttering and bestrewn. The bags and debris are an established part of the picture. They like it up there and prefer not to be disturbed.

Once, at a pedestrian mall between Roosevelt Avenue and Union Street in Queens, Tim and I were taking detritus out of some young linden trees growing in pots. The trees had been afflicted, years before, with a bondage of little holiday lights in strings. The lights had long ago quit working and had been abandoned rather than taken down. We were pretty sure they had no current anymore, but getting electrocuted via our aluminum poles was still a concern. I began on one tree and Tim on another, twenty yards or so away.

I noticed a dirty blue bath towel hanging between some branches. It seemed to bulge a bit; I figured it was full of water, as is a lot of trash in trees. With the hook of the snagger, I cut the bulge to drain it. Instantly a large rat sprang from the hole I'd made and shot down the pole at me. I remember seeing its teeth. It moved so fast it would have reached my hands before I let go of the pole, but at the last split second it leaped from the pole to another tree, scrabbled swiftly up, leaped to the roof of a building, and disappeared.

Even onlooking pigeons sometimes got upset with us and wanted us to leave well enough alone. As we wielded our pole, they would fly at us with keening, gurgling cries.

In Collect Pond Park, on Centre Street downtown, we were trying to remove a pigeon that had caught its foot in a piece of party balloon wrapped around a high branch – that ribbon is like wire, and the pigeon, unable to free itself, had died – and as we were maneuvering the pole closer suddenly all the park's many pigeons began swooping near the corpse protectively and diving toward our heads. Soon a riot of pigeons filled the high, narrow shaft formed by the gloomy government buildings looming around. We ended up leaving the body where it was.

Among the city's human occupants, a few seemed to like what we were doing. Now and then, windows in an apartment building overlooking a tree we were debagging would go up, and a resident would lean out and applaud. A nice elderly lady might call down and invite us in for a tuna sandwich and a glass of grape juice; an old man once thanked me and gave me a dollar. Or else people said things to us like, "Thank God the city is finally doing something about this problem." Other observers, naturally, heckled us and told us we were idiots. By the Walt Whitman housing projects, in Brooklyn, someone dropped a forty-ounce beer bottle from an upper window to a point on the lawn uncomfortably near us. When I tried to describe bag snagging to some black and Latino students in a class I visited at Kingsborough Community College, a lot of them were offended that anyone could devote time to an activity so (to them) pointless and unnecessary.

At home, the reaction of our wives to our newfound pastime was what Alice Kramden's would have been to a

similar scheme of Ralph's. This reaction grew more pronounced during the period when some of the objects we
removed from trees seemed so interesting to us that we
began bringing them home. I got a sense of the opinion of
wives in general one afternoon when I'd spent the day indoors with domestic duties and took a break by doing some
snagging on my own in Prospect Park and vicinity. When I
came back, our downstairs neighbor, Chris Avanzino, happened to be standing on the stoop, her baby on her hip. She
looked me over and said, "Your wife is in there taking care
of your two-year-old kid with a hundred-and-two-degree
temperature and you're walking around the neighborhood
with a pole taking bags out of *trees* … " She shook her head
and gave me a pitying, soul-withering smile.

Our pursuit of bag snagging led down various paths –
for example, into the obscurities of patent law. Tim and I
thought our snagger might be patentable, because probably
no device like it had ever existed before. Our first patent
attorney, a calm, bald man named Charlie Blank, said he
thought our chances of getting a patent were good. Then
he retired. Another attorney at Charlie Blank's firm took
over our application, and a year or two later told us that
the Patent and Trademark Office had rejected it because
a fruit picker patented in 1869 duplicated our snagger's
function – something to do with a similar hook on the

end of the fruit picker. Our attorney appealed the decision, on the grounds that the fruit picker would not work as effectively on plastic bags, which in any event did not exist back in 1869. This time, the patent office agreed and issued us US Patent NO 5,566,538. *The New York Times* selected our snagger for mention in its weekly "Patents" column, along with a surgical tool that uses a tiny beam of water moving at supersonic speed to cut human eye tissue. We were delighted to get the patent – it's like a small asterisk of immortality.

Partly because of the patent, and through a set of other circumstances too complicated to go into, I appeared in a movie, *Blue in the Face* (Miramax, 1995, starring Harvey Keitel), in a cameo role as myself talking about bags in trees. The movie did not do very well. In the art theater where I saw it, I was the only person in the auclience. The host of a radio show in New York happened to see the movie, however, and he asked Bill and Tim and me to be on his show. The husband of Bette Midler, the singer and movie star, heard the broadcast and afterward called the radio station and asked if we would sell him a bag snagger as a birthday present for his wife. Bette Midler, as people know, is an enemy of litter, and she shares our opinion of bags in trees. Bette Midler liked the snagger her husband gave her and eventually she bought more of them for the cleanup crew she sponsors in the city, and the hardworking kids who staff it began to make a real dent in uptown bags in trees.

With the hope of selling a lot more bag snaggers, we formed a company, Bag Snaggers, INC. A man in California

who has a small business manufacturing and selling spe-
cialty poles – tree-pruning poles, snake-lassoing poles,
monkey-catching poles for use in airplane cargo hangars
when monkeys escape from shipping crates and climb up
into the rafters – agreed to manufacture our snagger and
interlocking fiberglass poles to go with it. We listed ourselves in some public-works Web sites and catalogs, and
sold a few sets to civic groups and municipalities. Bill, who
handled the paperwork, began referring to Bag Snaggers,
INC, as a "multi-hundred-dollar company." But, over time,
our sales were not brisk. The park employees and ground-
skeepers of America evidently are not keen on shelling out
for a tool that will involve them in new duties wrangling
debris out of trees. Recently, Bill and Tim and I have been
talking about dissolving the company and shutting opera-
tions down.

    The truth is, these days we don't go bag snagging as
much as we used to. None of us live in the city anymore;
Tim moved his jewelry business to Great Barrington,
Massachusetts, I moved to Montana and then New Jersey,
and Bill was in New Jersey all along. We have families and
the usual excess of more important obligations. A morning
of bag snagging requires logistics and scheduling and phone
calls. Plus, when we started doing this we were younger;
reaching sixty feet of wobbly fiberglass into a tree and snagging a bag amid obstructing branches can be vexingly hard.

We've begun to get bag-snagging injuries – shoulder, neck, back – and around the house the sympathy available for them is only the negative kind. We hoped that a new group of young guys would see the appeal of our tree-bag pursuit and take over, but so far that hasn't happened. Apparently, bag-snagging fever was specific just to us, and just to then.

Stuff having to do with bag snagging still comes up. People think of bags in trees, and they think of us. An aid worker just back from Africa tells us that there's a lot of debris in trees in the poorer parts of Africa, and the closer you get to the supposed epicenter of the AIDS epidemic the more of it there is. An Irishwoman says that in Ireland bags in trees are called "witches' knickers." A resident of the Upper East Side writes to tell us that ever since some balloons got stuck in a tree outside her bedroom window her family has had bad luck with health; she asks if we can take the balloons out, and one afternoon we do. We still accept special requests occasionally.

At a midtown cocktail party a while ago, Thomas Mallon, the novelist, asked me if we still took bags out of trees. I said we did, and he said he had a related problem: helium-filled Mylar balloons that float to the ceiling of Grand Central Station and linger there for months. He asked if there was anything we could do about this. I said I would check it out.

The next time I was in Grand Central, I saw what he meant. The vaulted ceiling of the main concourse rises a hundred feet or more above the station's marble floor. The height is lofty but still measurable in human terms – it's the heart-stopping altitude of the tightrope walker, the altitude of prophetic ascension and rocket liftoff. When visitors come into the station for the first time, their eyes go to the ceiling, and, in the vast interior space the ceiling encloses, their prospects seem to expand. Looking up in Grand Central evokes feelings of vertigo and excitement and fear of heights and dizziness and exaltation that may recall the reasons you moved to New York City in the first place. The ceiling is the dark greenish-blue of a clear summer-night sky, studded with small lights representing stars in the constellations of the zodiac, with the figures of the zodiac outlined in off-white around them. And there in the middle of the ceiling – in the constellation of Pisces – was a shiny, silver, heart-shaped Mylar balloon.

I came back week after week and kept tabs on it. It moved only slightly, between the ventral fins of one of Pisces's fish. Once, I was there in July and a tour guide leading a group said in annoyance that the balloon had been up there since Valentine's Day. A Metro-North worker standing by a track entrance said that tourists had just complained to him about the balloon ruining their photographs. By then, thousands or millions of Grand Central passersby must have seen it. In this most public of American public spaces, the balloon was unreachable, top of the world, thumb in your eye.

Obviously we could not get to it with bag-snagging poles. Even if we braced the poles with some kind of tripod, the ceiling is too high. From a guy who works for the Bryant Park conservancy, Bill heard that a cook from the Oyster Bar restaurant, on the lower level of the station, used to shoot balloons down at night with a BB gun when he got off work, but to me shooting seemed too much of a risk to the recently restored zodiac paintings, as well as not quite sporting, somehow. And then there are the Homeland Security soldiers who patrol the station with their M-16s ...

So we thought about it, and here's the idea: get three other helium balloons at a florist's or party store; cover the balloons with double-sided tape, judiciously, so as not to affect their buoyancy; tie the tape-covered balloons to stout monofilament line on a fishing rod; stand beneath the balloon lodged on the ceiling; send the retriever balloons aloft until they touch the other balloon; nudge them around until the tape adheres; then reel the retrievers and their tape-stuck captive back down.

Recently, Bill and I ran a field test of this idea under a tall highway bridge in the Jersey Meadowlands. First, we sent up a target balloon on a long lead. It came to a stop between two girders. Then we sent the retrievers. Despite a brisk wind (which, of course, would be absent in Grand Central), the retriever balloons reached the target balloon, nestled around it with a kind of natural gregariousness, stuck to it with the double-sided tape, and held it securely enough so that we could reel them and it down. Repeated tests achieved the same result. Man, the toolmaker: at our success the marshy New Jersey landscape stretched around us in submission, like background scenery in a portrait of Sir Isaac Newton. This idea can work, we are 100 percent sure. Whenever we get the go-ahead from the company that manages Grand Central, we're ready. ❦

ZHUANGZI

Horses' Hoofs*

This essay is one of the most devastating attacks on civilization and Confucianism. But one should not forget Chuangtse's [Zhuangzi's] positive dictum that the aim of government and philosophy should be to "let the people live out the even tener of their lives" and that "all creation shall be able to fulfill their instincts of life [the laws of their nature]."

—editorial note by the translator, Lin Yutang

*H*ORSES HAVE HOOFS to carry them over frost and snow, and hair to protect them from wind and cold. They eat grass and drink water, and fling up their tails and gallop. Such is the real nature of horses. Ceremonial halls and big dwellings are of no use to them.

One day Polo† appeared, saying, "I am good at managing horses." So he burned their hair and clipped them, and

---

* From the *Zhuangzi*. Translated and edited by Lin Yutang, in the collection *The Importance of Understanding: translations from the Chinese* (World Publishing Co., 1960). The editorial introduction and footnotes were all provided by Lin Yutang.

† Sun Yang, 658-619 BCE, famous horse trainer.

pared their hoofs and branded them. He put halters around
their necks and shackles around their legs and numbered
them according to their stables. The result was that two
or three in every ten died. Then he kept them hungry and
thirsty, trotting them and galloping them, and taught them
to run in formations, with the misery of the tasseled bridle
in front and the fear of the knotted whip behind, until more
than half of them died.

The potter says, "I am good at managing clay. If I want
it round, I use compasses; if rectangular, a square." The
carpenter says, "I am good at managing wood. If I want it
curved, I use an arc; if straight, a line." But on what grounds
can we think that the nature of clay and wood desires this
application of compasses and square, and arc and line?
Nevertheless, every age extols Polo for his skill in training
horses, and potters and carpenters for their skill with clay
and wood. Those who manage [govern] the affairs of the
empire make the same mistake.

I think one who knows how to govern the empire should
not do so. For the people have certain natural instincts –
to weave and clothe themselves, to till the fields and feed
themselves. This is their common character, in which all
share. Such instincts may be called "heaven-born". So in the
days of perfect nature, men were quiet in their movements
and serene in their looks. At that time, there were no paths
over mountains, no boats or bridges over waters. All things
were produced, each in its natural district. Birds and beasts
multiplied; trees and shrubs thrived. Thus it was that birds
and beasts could be led by the hand, and one could climb

up and peep into the magpie's nest. For in the days of perfect nature, man lived together with birds and beasts, and there was no distinction of their kind. Who could know of the distinctions between gentlemen and common people? Being all equally without knowledge, their virtue could not go astray. Being all equally without desires, they were in a state of natural integrity. In this state of natural integrity, the people did not lose their [original] nature.

And then when sages appeared, crawling for charity and limping with duty, doubt and confusion entered men's minds. They said they must make merry by means of music and enforce distinctions by means of ceremony, and the empire became divided against itself. Were the uncarved wood not cut up, who could make sacrificial vessels? Were white jade left uncut, who could make the regalia of courts? Were Tao and virtue not destroyed, what use would there be for charity and duty? Were men's natural instincts not lost, what need would there be for music and ceremonies? Were the five colors not confused, who would need decorations? Were the five notes not confused, who would adopt the six pitch-pipes? Destruction of the natural integrity of things for the production of articles of various kinds – this is the fault of the artisan. Destruction of Tao and virtue in order to introduce charity and duty – this is the error of the sages. Horses live on dry land, eat grass, and drink water. When pleased, they rub their necks together. When angry, they turn around and kick up their heels at each other. Thus far only do their natural instincts carry them. But bridled and bitted, with a moon-shaped metal plate on their foreheads, they learn to cast vicious looks, to turn their heads to bite, to nudge at the yoke, to cheat the bit out of their mouths or steal the bridle off their heads. Thus their minds and gestures become like those of thieves. This is the fault of Polo.

In the days of Ho Shu,[*] the people did nothing in particular at their homes and went nowhere in particular in their walks. Having food, they rejoiced; tapping their bellies, they wandered about. Thus far the natural capacities of the people carried them. The sages came then to make them bow and bend with ceremonies and music, in order to regulate the external forms of intercourse, and dangled charity and duty before them, in order to keep their minds in submission. Then the people began to labor and develop a taste for knowledge, and to struggle with one another in their desire for gain, to which there is no end. This is the error of the sages. ᴄᴋ

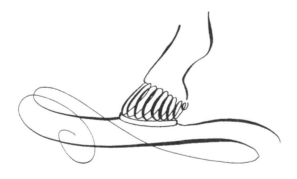

---

*   A mythical ruler.

ANDREW WILLSON

On the Sincerity of Irony

IRONY: A mode of speech in which the meaning is contrary
to the words.
—Entry in Dr. Johnson's dictionary

Consider the cat's use of its front claws. Rather, consider
the cat's use of its paws once the claws have been removed.
What does it do with them, those blunt paws and phantom
claws?

My mother had her cat declawed when she got her
from the pound. But the cat, being two years old, was accustomed to spreading her front paws whenever she wanted
and unleashing those talons she'd been born with. I still
remember the cat's hangdog look when my mother brought
her home from the vet with her front paws wrapped in
bandages. She didn't move or meow for days.

That was five years ago. But I don't think the cat's ever
really gotten over her loss. She routinely puts her front
paws up against something – the couch, a box, your leg –
and shuffles them back and forth as if she were trying to
scratch or grab hold. Surely, she must have noticed that
her claws are gone by now. Perhaps its an ironic gesture.

Maybe when she looks like she's trying to scratch my leg, she's actually showing affection.

On prom night of my junior year of high school, when I saw my girlfriend in that lime-green dress for the first time, feelings of love, tenderness, and desire were tumbling around my insides. The idea of saying "you look beautiful" or "pretty" or (worst of all) "nice" seemed like flimsy praise. So instead I said, "Baby, you look so ... *ugly.*" She punched me, of course, but smiled even as she unclenched her fist. She knew: a word of irony was the best choice, because any word of adolescent praise or love, no matter how earnestly spoken, couldn't have done justice to the spin-cycle that my internal organs were going through. Besides, I knew it would make her laugh ... eventually.

Perhaps the cat, in a swell of affection, can find no better way to show her love than by pretending to scratch my leg – as if an ironic, clawless clawing expresses affection better than the sincere nuzzle. Perhaps it's something else entirely: a deep expression of frustration, resentment, or anger – an acknowledgment of and railing against her condition, like an inmate's futile shaking of the bars or Lear's naked fist wagging at the relentless heavens. Maybe she's just downright pissed at us for putting her through the surgical violence of declawing and then cooping her up in a suburban apartment. She does, after all, still try to run out the front door every time it opens.

At present, the cat is curled up asleep on a chair, her clawless paw draped over her eyes and her heavy breaths sounding with a purr of satisfaction. No, this furball looks to be free of frustration and hate. Then again, Saul Bellow listened to the chirps of birds and heard "abysmal depths of aggression, which only Man – Stupid Man – heard as innocence." Well, if the birds are full of aggression I suppose their predator, the cat, might be all the more aggressive in those dreams beyond her purr? What kind of a four-legged psychopath might my mother be living with?

A well-developed sense of irony? Or a gnawing sense of imprisonment and frustration? A feline Voltaire? Or a feline Gore Vidal? Why the either/or, as if ironic affection and sincere frustration are mutually exclusive? To a certain degree I probably use irony not only to be funny or to show affection, but also out of a deep sense of frustration – likely a frustration with the false earnestness of others and with the difficulty (more accurately, the Herculean labor) of precise and vivid linguistic self-expression. Rainer Maria Rilke, who addresses the subject in *Letters to a Young Poet*, would probably say that irony is the petulant and sneering child born to minds that are frustrated with their own inability to contemplate "the depth of things." Rilke cautions his young correspondent against irony: "Do not let yourself be governed by it." He does go on to say that if an "ironic attitude springs from a necessity of your nature" you should "strengthen it into a stern instrument" and allow it to "take its place in the series of tools with which you will have to shape your art," but on the whole his message is clear: abstain from irony.

If Rilke dislikes ironic verse, he loathes the ironic person, who, in his view, is like Oscar Wilde's cynic: the man who knows the price of everything but the value of nothing. Rilke claims that the cure for irony is to "seek the depth of things" because "thither irony never descends"; irony shrivels to something "small and helpless" in the face of "great and serious objects". He suggests that an ironic perception of the world derives from a blindness to the value of higher things. Irony, according to Rilke, is not simply an aspect of language; it is an obfuscating sickness – the soul's version of cataracts.

If Rilke is right, then my own soul's vision is likely clouded by irony, as evidenced by the fact that I suspect irony in the cat's behavior. I judge the behavior of others based mainly on what I know of myself. I remember the day when that was made clear to me. A friend needed to entrust me with his wallet for an hour, but before he handed it to me he opened it up and counted the money. Once he was gone I remarked to another friend that I was a little offended by that casual display of mistrust. My friend looked at me and said, "He didn't mean anything by it. He only did that because he knew that he'd steal *your* money if he had the chance." Just as this friend saw a potential thief in everyone, so I see the potential for irony in every creature (two legs or four) that I come across.

So I have an ironic attitude. Is that so bad? Rilke admits that irony can be a good tool for writers to have in their repertoire ("if it really innately belongs to you," that is), and I do, after all, like to write. Many great writers – Chaucer, Montaigne, Austen, and Swift, to name a few – make frequent use of irony. But is it any good for life?

Rilke cautions us to be wary of it "especially in uncreative moments". Now there are certainly those enviable people who seem never to experience an uncreative moment: the Schuberts and Joyces of the world, for instance, who have left scores of napkinless cafes in their wake, or John Updike, who has a sentence to show for every hour of his life. But what about me? I've drunk millions of cups of coffee without writing a word. My uncreative moments last for weeks at a time. Given that my life isn't one constant act of creation, what should I do with the excess irony, with the wry perceptions that don't find their way onto paper? If I don't give up on it then I might, in Rilke's words, get "too familiar with it", or irony and I might develop a "growing intimacy". In fifty years I'll likely be an old, bitter cynic. To my mind the most horrifying piece of literature is not *Macbeth* or *The Tell-Tale Heart* or the like; it is Johnson's *Life of Swift*, a portrait of a man whose keen sense of irony gradually transmogrifies into an inability to perceive anything but the loathsome and disgusting. Johnson says of Swift that he eventually became so cynical and cantankerous that his "asperity, continually increasing, condemned him to solitude; and his resentment of solitude sharpened his asperity." Had Swift been alive to read Hazlitt's "On the Pleasure of Hating," I think he would have felt sympathy with the essay's resounding coda: "Have I not reason to hate and despise myself? Indeed I do; and chiefly for not having hated and despised the world enough."

In my last year of college, I took two fiction writing courses. Looking back I'm struck by the fact that most of the stories I wrote were about old or middle-aged men. And nearly every one of those men was cynical and bitter, or, as Philip Larkin puts it, a specimen of those "old-type natural fouled-up guys". My justification for not writing about people my own age was that young people have so little to lose – they have nothing at stake. (I realize now, however, that at stake is the future – at stake is everything.) But when I recently heard Martin Amis say that writers, whether they know it or not, often write about what scares them most, I knew I'd found a likely reason for the prevalence of the cynically old and middle-aged in my stories. I am afraid that one day my reticence to say "beautiful" will lead to blindness to beauty itself, afraid that an ironic youth is but a long slide into decades darkened and distorted by cynicism.

This fear isn't one that I've developed in a vacuum either. Aside from Rilke's short paragraph, entire books, such as Jedediah Purdy's *For Common Things: Irony, Trust, and Commitment in America Today*, have been devoted to discussing irony's erosive effect on the higher human attributes like conviction. While Purdy does attempt to make a distinction between cynics and ironists – ironists, he says, do not mingle at parties but make wry comments in the corner while cynics refuse to go to parties at all – his descriptions of irony ultimately differ little from cynicism:

> The point of irony is a quiet refusal to believe in the depth of relationships, the sincerity of motivation, or the truth of speech – especially earnest speech. In place of the

romantic idea that each of us harbors a true self struggling for expression, the ironist offers the suspicion that
we are just quantum selves – all spin, all the way down.

Strike "offers the suspicion", insert "is convinced", and you
have a card-carrying cynic. As suspicion precedes conviction, irony precedes cynicism.

If this is indeed the case, then maybe irony is best left
to literature alone and omitted from the rest of life entirely.
Irony, Rilke says, is a valid tool for literature. But isn't it the
way of certain tools that once they are removed from their
usual workspaces and used in unintended ways they cause
nothing but damage? Hammers and nails and saws, for
instance, build great spice racks, but when they come out
of the shed and into the house, what comes of it but blood,
screams, and stories for the six o'clock news? Irony makes
for effective writing – it looks good on paper – but maybe
when it's used in the world of the living it makes for little
else but alienation, first from the things we should value
the most (beauty, art, love and loved ones) and eventually,
as with Swift, from everything.

Ultimately, however, I cannot accept that irony – in
literature or life – devalues our relationships or sincerity
or truth or the struggle for expression or any other human
good. Exactly the opposite, I think nothing is more sincere
than irony. It actually protects the very things that Purdy
says it devalues.

In fact, I think that sincerity, in the absence of irony,
can not only be self-defeating but can even devalue our

nobler concepts. I once met a man who, in the course of a single conversation, told me that he *loves* his dog, he *loves* his wife, he *loves* golf, he *loves* CNN, he *loves* Proust, he *loves* cheese, and he *loves* new socks. To which I thought, "And I just *love* your sincerity." This "lover" of all things had through the very earnestness of his speech caused me to doubt his sincerity. He made love seem puny. To be clear, I don't doubt that he was and is a very earnest man (indeed, there wasn't so much as an ironic tooth in his candid, always-moving mouth). I'm sure that he is capable of love. I simply question his sincerity when, with equal seriousness, he claims to love such disparate things. Granted, love is an extraordinarily elastic concept, but the day that it applies in the same way to both your spouse and your socks is the day that poets should throw out their pens and paper. That man needs a strong injection of irony. When sincerity is left unchecked by irony and dominates the way a person speaks, it dilutes, denigrates even, the very concepts and feelings it ostensibly upholds. Irony, in fact, protects sincerity by acting as its necessary balance.

When I was thirteen my mother, sister, and I met our extended family for a most exquisite dinner at McDonald's. As a kid my palette registered nothing besides fat, sugar, and salt, so I had no reservations about eating fast food. But I was troubled by something else that happened there. We were all seated with our food on trays, but before we were allowed to start eating we had to pray as a family. First we collectively began with a standard prayer ("Come Lord Jesus be our guest, and let thy gifts to us be blessed"), and then my uncle soloed about our gratitude for the food and the chance to meet as a family, after which we closed in unison with "Amen" – everyone except me, that is. Something about the idea of praying over fast food left me even queasier than the fries did. I refused to take part. When my family closed their eyes in reverence, I rolled my eyes in frustration and took a bite out of my sandwich. While they prayed, I was thinking a less articulate version of this: "Heavenly Father, thank you for the bounty of thy value menu and for the plenitude of thy fries. Thanks be to you also, dearest Jesus, for the refills of Pepsi I will obtaineth from thy soda fountain everflowing. Thy disposable paper cup, oh Lord, truly hath no bottom." If they are so quick to lavish prayers on Big Macs and Big Gulps, I had to wonder, what language will they have left to express awe or more profound feelings of gratitude? What would they do, for instance, if a new child was born into the family? Pray over it? Just as they prayed over their greasy, mass-produced, plastic-wrapped hunks of carcinogenic non-food. I suspected that they weren't sanctifying themselves or their "meal"; they were simply cheapening prayer.

Perhaps the ironist's suspicion could turn into the cynic's conviction, but is the over-earnest person really any better off? Half of being a cynic, according to Wilde, stems from being unable to recognize value. So in my moments of irony I am perhaps halfway to cynicism: I often avoid words of great value, the weightier words in English, it is true. But only because I am aware that there is a cost to overuse. Meanwhile, what does the man who loves everything indiscriminately recognize of value? Maybe the truth, then, is that we are all about halfway to becoming cynics, that to avoid Swift's fate we all must balance our awareness of values and costs as diligently as we do our checkbooks.

  When my mother's cat has finished her dinner she often puts her blunt paws against my leg and begins her clawless scratching. At first I think it's cute – that this is her way of thanking me – until I recall the scene from *The Silence of the Lambs* in which Hannibal Lecter attacks his guards precisely after they've fed him. More seriously, however, it occurs to me that she uses her declawed paws in much the same way that I use irony. We both feign the use of something we were born with but lost: claws on her part, the unquestioning sincerity of childhood on mine. I'm sure there was a time when I, too, said I "loved" everything with complete earnestness, but that earnestness has been snuffed out, bit by bit, with each birthday candle. I have not given up on sincere expression simply because childlike earnestness is gone. But now I have to rely on irony in its place. Purdy tries to convince his readers that irony refutes the idea that "each of us harbors a true self struggling for expression." I have observed the opposite. The cat keeps up her clawless clawing in an endless experiment to find the best use of her paws, and I keep using irony in a struggle to find the most sincere means of expression. ✒

DAVID MAMET

Knives*

I CAN'T ABIDE stainless steel. It gives me the fantods.

I will accept it in a toaster, but I can't see that it has any place in the blade of a knife.

W. Grigg used to work for Randall's in Orlando, and he offered, first through them and then independently, the finest Daddy Barlow I've ever seen. It was massive – had a lockback that walked and talked as if it were made for NASA, ivory scales, and, unfortunately, a stainless steel blade. It reduced the status of the knife, for me, from that of a superb tool to that of a superb artifact – like a down-filled Hawaiian shirt. What has "progress" brought us to?

What in the world, I ask, is the stuff good for?

Compare today's stainless sheath and pocket knives with the universally available mass-market products of the twenties and thirties, and it makes one want to cry.

Those old, gray-mottled blades would *cut*. (I've got one in my pocket now, a Victorian Joseph Rodgers four-blade congress jack. Dirty stag scales, stained and worn blades, but I can put an edge on it, and it will shave hairs.)

The stainless steel knife just doesn't feel right to me.

---

* From *Jafsie and John Henry: essays* (Free Press, 1999).

I put it on a stone and feel like I'm trying to sharpen the front fender of a Chevy. It just doesn't want to cooperate.

But, then, I was ruined from the first. I bought one of those eleven-dollar Russell belt knives out of the Herter's catalogue in the fifties, and that was and is a knife. Great steel, shaped to the hand, no guard, just the blade and full tang, with the wood scales riveted on. I found a replacement three years ago at the Morrisville Gun Show for four bucks, and I treasure it.

The only other real bargain I ever found was at a trading venue called Mud City near Stowe some fifteen years back. There was a Russell Daddy Barlow in bone, in what I'd call excellent shape, for three dollars. I used it for a year, and then sold it through the mail to a well-known trader, and soon thereafter saw it on the cover of a knife magazine. Wish I'd kept it. Oh well.

I was sick some years ago, and laid up in bed with, for some reason, a knife magazine on the bedside table; and to pass the time I wrote away to all the custom makers mentioned therein, and, eventually, did business with a few of them.

Notable among the lot was Bill Bagwell, who became a friend and hunting companion (as I look across at the Glenwood stove I see beneath it a Bagwell-marked goat's-head fire poker he made me one evening at the forge out back of his east Texas home).

Bill ruined me for both stainless steel and the stock-removal method (making knives by grinding down the metal blank).

I've watched Bill forge his knives by hand, packing the

blade here, lightening it there, and watched them cut, and they're no joke. One of his more dramatic demonstrations consists in tying four one-inch-diameter rods together and hacking through the four with one swipe of a bowie.

He has also been kind enough to give me sharpening lessons, for which I am grateful.

Like many knife-makers (like many crafts people, for that matter), Bill is a contrarian. He sharpens a blade in a manner exactly opposite to that which I (and you) have been told and have read in every magazine and pamphlet. He drags the blade *away* from the cutting edge, until it turns over a wire edge onto the reverse side, and then *very* gently wipes the wire edge off.

And then he uses the knife to chop through a two-by-six, and then shave hairs.

Quite a demonstration. Which brings us back to the purpose of the instrument in the first place. It's meant to cut.

If the knife won't take an edge, if it won't *hold* an edge, why in the world would one carry it? I believe many of us have had the experience of being in the woods and shaving a stick or two for kindling and finding the knife dull. What a maddening bore, and how it widens one's vocabulary.

And a pocketknife can always be relied on in the woods, if for nothing else than to get itself lost.

I grew up in the era just predating that of the Buckknife, and have never quite been able to reconcile myself to the belt-sheath for a pocketknife. The idea reminds me of the German Forester's Knife – the folding sheath knife so beloved of the European mind.

I say get in or get out. If it's a sheath knife, wear it on a sheath. If it's a folding knife, put it in a pocket.

Yes, it eventually *will* get lost, but in the meantime you don't have to walk around looking like Mr. Peepers, with the cutlery equivalent of the pocket-protector on your belt.

The pocketknife should be in the pocket. The Victorians said one gentleman should never ask "Have you the time?" or "May I borrow your knife" of another; he should have his own knife and watch. And I concur. Carry the pocketknife in the pocket, and when it goes missing, get another one.

Most junk shops, and low-end antique stores, have a display case in which one can find a good, cheap old non-stainless pocketknife.

There are a lot of people making lovely custom folders. I've had a few myself, and first they end up in the wash, and then they end up on the moon with eighteen minutes of Rosemary Woods' tapes.

When I started collecting one could see, at a mid-level New York antique show, Wostenholn and Rodgers bowie knives, emblazoned DEATH TO SLAVERY, DEATH TO ABOLITION, HUNTER'S COMPANION, CALIFORNIA KNIFE, and all the other mottos of the Victorian export trade – beautiful pieces of history for a few hundred dollars. And I still kick myself. I didn't buy them. One could see the Will and Fink San Francisco daggers, or prostitute's knives, Wade and Butcher folding dirks, and so on; which articles have now gone to visit the Quality in the museums, or the Butterfield arms auction.

My collection is a bit more utilitarian. I've got some

good R. H. Ruana pieces, a couple of Marbles IDEAL, a Remington UMC on the same pattern (perhaps it was made by Marbles), hunting knives, camp knives, and bowies from Mr. Bagwell, and a box full of old folders, unremarkable save for the IXL pearl-handled advertising knife, which has gone missing, and an ivory-scaled Victorian gentleman's knife, which I just opened before me.

This is the finest pocketknife I've ever seen. It has a three-inch lockback main blade in a modified spear, a penblade, a corkscrew, a buttonhook, an awl, toothpick, scissors, nail file, and tweezers. It all fits together in rather a sleeveboard pattern, and the silver escutcheon plate is inscribed "Sir H. H. Pollock, Bart."

And it is cute as a button, and almost might make one entertain the notion of a belt-sheath for a pocketknife. It is marked "Thomas Turner and Co. Suffolk Works," and it is pretty damned sweet. The accoutrements fit in tightly and unobtrusively, and are made for use.

It is the opposite of the Swiss Army knives, those all-purpose instruments which seem to be handy for anything save cutting.

I am not a fan of the multipurpose tool. The genre seems to me, in the main, 'morphadite rigs which might do a bit of a few jobs, and then contribute to the entertainment of the situation by breaking.

An exception: I remember Randall's used to advertise (their current literature advises me they still do) that they would fit a small compass into a knife's butt-cap – a style pioneered by Bradford Angier, I believe. I thought this rather a *cheechako* affectation until the first time I got myself no-joke lost in the woods. Currently I think there is no pocket or tool which would not be improved by the addendum of a compass.

But, finally, both the beauty and the utility of any instrument depend on the single-mindedness and talent of the designer in fitting the tool to the task.

Which brings us back to philosophy. I can use my pocketknives as handy lifters to open the woodstove; when I carried a Buckknife I found the brass bolster made a good hammer; the Swiss Army knife is, as we know, great for removing a splinter, but, at the end of the day, the purpose of a knife is to cut. To that end it should be made of steel designed to cut, it should be (preferably) forged and/or ground into a shape suitable for the sort of cutting intended, and the blade should be set in a handle ergonomically correct for the tasks at hand.

Mr. Bagwell advises (and carries) a large (nine-to-twelve-inch) bowie in the woods. It is not a macho overcompensation. It's not there to skin deer or to dissuade or subdue malefactors, it's a substitute for the hand ax, and it does the job right smartly. For the camp chores, including skinning, he carries a five- or six-inch camp knife, and so do I.

I'm talking about a small, single-edged (probably droppoint) narrow-tang utility knife, with, probably, a halfguard. It can whittle a fuzz-tree, or a tent peg, lift a pot off the fire, or dress a deer, and how many other tools can make that statement?·

We all have various clothing and gear that looks pretty, but we take items into the woods because we're confident in them, and if they don't function as required, we don't take them again. So I take a Bagwell camp knife, and slip a traitorous pocketknife into a pocket or two, and, probably, put an old Marbles Safety Ax into the pack. (The bowie knife, I do allow, does the job better, but we all saw too many articles in too many magazines over the years by a chap who dressed out an elk with a pocket comb; and I wouldn't want to meet that fellow on the trail and feel called upon to explain myself. Is this a character defect? Definitely.)

On the city street I slip an old Robeson or Rodgers, or a Case Serpentine jack, into a pocket. (All my custom-folders – Cenofante, Bagwell-Pardue, Teruzola, etc. – as I said, have ended on the Moon.)

A word about browsing.

As a kid I enjoyed the gun-and-knife rooms at Marshall Field's Men's Store and, down Wabash Avenue, at Abercrombie and Fitch/V.L.+A, at which last store I bought my first Randall knife out of the case – a bird-and-trout knife, long since gone. I am pleased to note and to report that the same spirit of informed and friendly assistance I found then seems to live on at Stoddards Cutlery in Boston, at Paragon Sports knife department in New York, through Bruce Voyles, and through A.G. Russell's various mail-order enterprises, and at the New York Custom Knife Show – some modern and urban versions of the Courthouse Lawn.

I've enjoyed collecting knives. I wish I'd kept an example of the Grigg Daddy Barlow I decried at the beginning. It was a work of art.

I wish I'd bought that California bowie at the New York Knife Show, and the decrepit, rusted Randall fighter a fellow had for sale in Hyder, Alaska. It was coming apart, the leather washers were eaten through, but it had been around, and the sheath was marked H. HEISER. We differed by five dollars, and the knife is probably still up there.

What would I have done with it? I would have sent it to Randall's, asked them to refurbish it, carried it once or twice. Someone might say it would then be forgotten in my closet rather than living in my memory.

I like a knife that will stain. I like it to show wear. I like it to have a story — that, after all, is the joy of collecting, to understand the story. The joy of use is to add to it. ❧

E. B. WHITE

Memorandum*

TODAY I SHOULD CARRY the pumpkins and squash from the back porch to the attic. The nights are too frosty to leave them outdoors any longer. And as long as I am making some trips to the attic I should also take up the boat cushions and the charts and the stuff from the galley and also a fishing rod that belongs up in the attic. Today I should finish filling in the trench we dug for the water pipe and should haul two loads of beach gravel from the Naskeag bar to spread on top of the clay fill. And I should stop in and pay the Reverend Mr. Smith for the gravel I got a month or two ago and ask him if he has seen a bear.

I ought to finish husking the corn and wheel the old stalks out and dump them on the compost pile, and while I am out there I should take a fork and pitch over the weeds that were thrown at the edge of the field last August and rake the little windfalls from under the apple tree and pitch them on to the heap too. I ought to go down to the shore at dead low water and hook on to the mooring with a chain and make the chain fast to the float, so that the tide will

---

* From *One Man's Meat* (Harper & Bros., 1944).

pick up the mooring rock and I can tow the whole thing ashore six hours later. I ought to knock the wedges out from the frames of the pier, put a line on the frames, and tow them in on the high water. First, though, I would have to find a line long enough to tie every frame. If I'm to do any work at the shore I ought first to put a cement patch on the leak in my right boot. After the frames are on the beach another fellow and myself ought to carry them up and stack them. And there is probably enough rockweed on the beach now so that I ought to bring up a load or two for the sheep shed. I ought to find out who it is that is shooting coot down in the cove today, just to satisfy my own curiosity. He was out before daybreak with his decoys, but I do not think he has got any birds.

I ought to take up the wire fence round the chicken range today, roll it up in bundles, tie them with six-thread, and store them at the edge of the woods. Then I ought to move the range houses off the field and into the corner of the woods and set them up on blocks for the winter, but I ought to sweep them out first and clean the roosts with a wire brush. It would be a good idea to have a putty knife in my pocket, for scraping. I ought to add a bag of phosphate to the piles of hen dressing that have accumulated under the range houses and spread the mixture on the field, to get it ready for plowing. And I ought to decide whether to plow just the range itself or to turn over a little more on the eastern end. On my way in from the range I ought to stop at the henhouse long enough to climb up and saw off an overhanging branch from the apple tree – it might tear the paper roof in the first big wind storm. I shall have to get a ladder of course and a saw.

Today I certainly ought to go over to the mill and get four twelve-inch boards, twelve feet long and half an inch thick, to use in building three new hoppers for dry mash feeding to my pullets. They are now laying seventy-eight per cent and giving me about eighty dozen eggs a week. I should also get one board that would be an inch thick, for the end pieces and for making the ends of the reels. I shouldn't need anything for the stands because I have enough stuff round the place to build the stands – which I had better make twenty-three inches high from floor to perch. If I were to make them less than that, the birds on the floor would pick at the vents of the birds feeding.

I ought to get some shingle nails and some spikes while I am at it, as we are out of those things. And I ought to sharpen the blade of my plane if I am going to build some hoppers. I ought to take the cutting-off saw and have it filed, as long as I am going over to the mill anyway. On the way back I ought to stop in at Frank Hamilton's house and put in my application for government lime and super, because I shall be passing his house and might just as well take advantage of it. Frank will ask me to sit down and talk a while, I imagine.

It is high time I raked up the bayberry brush which has been lying in the pasture since the August mowing. This would be a good chance to burn it today because we have had a rain and it is safe to burn. But before burning it I ought to find out whether it is really better for the pasture to burn stuff like that or to let it rot for dressing. I suppose there is so much wood in it it wouldn't rot up quickly and should be burned. Besides, I was once told in high-school chemistry that no energy is ever lost to the world, and presumably the ashes from the fires will strengthen my pasture in their own way.

I ought to take the buck lamb out of the flock of lambs today, before he gets to work on the ewe lambs, because I don't want them to get bred. I don't know just where to put him, but I ought to decide that today, and put him there. I should send away today for some phenothiazine so that I can drench my sheep next week. It would probably be a good idea to try phenothiazine this time instead of copper sulphate, which just gets the stomach worms and doesn't touch the nodular worms or the large-mouth bowel worms. And I ought to close the big doors on the north side of the barn cellar and board them up and bank them, so that the place won't be draughty down there at night when the sheep come in, as they are beginning to do. I have been thinking I ought to enlarge the south door so that I won't lose any lambs next spring from the ewes jamming through the narrow single opening, and this would be the time to do that.

Today I ought to start rebuilding the racks in the sheep shed, to fix them so the sheep can't pull hay out and waste it. There is a way to do this, and I know the way. So I am all set. Also I ought to fix up the pigpen down there in the barn cellar too and sweeten it up with a coat of whitening, so that I can get the pig indoors, because the nights are pretty cold now. The trough will probably not have to be rebuilt this year because last year I put a zinc binding all around the edges of it. (But if I *shouldn't* get round to fixing up the pen I should at least carry a forkful of straw down to the house where the pig now is – I should at least do that.)

This would be a good day to put in a new light in the window in the woodshed, and also there is one broken in the shop and one in the henhouse, so the sensible thing would be to do them all at once, as long as I have the putty all worked up and the glass cutter out. I ought to hook up the stove in the shop today, and get it ready for winter use. And I ought to run up the road and see Bert and find out why he hasn't delivered the cord of slabwood he said he was going to bring me. At any rate, I ought to make a place in the cellar for it today, which will mean cleaning house down there a little and neating up, and finding a better place to keep my flats and fillers for my egg cases. Incidentally, I ought to collect eggs right now, so there won't be any breakage in the nests.

It just occurred to me that if I'm going to the mill today I ought to measure the truck and figure out what I shall need in the way of hardwood boards to build a set of side-boards and a headboard and a tailboard for my stakes. I ought to bring these boards back with me along with the pine for the hoppers. I shall need two bolts for the ends of each sideboard, and one bolt for the cleat in the middle, and two bolts for the ends of each of the head-and tailboards, and there will be three each of them, so that makes fifty-four bolts I shall need, and the stakes are about an inch and a half through and the boards will be three-quarters, so that makes two inches and a quarter, and allow another half inch for washer and nut. About a three-inch bolt would do it. I better get them today.

Another thing I ought to do is take that grass seed that the mice have been getting into in the barn and store it in a wash boiler or some pails or something. I ought to set some mousetraps tonight, I mustn't forget. I ought to set one upstairs, I guess, in the little northeast chamber where the pipe comes through from the set tubs in the back kitchen, because this is the Mouse Fifth Avenue, and it would be a good chance for a kill. I ought to gather together some old clothes and stuff for the rummage sale to raise money to buy books for the town library, and I ought to rake the barnyard and wheel the dressing down into the barn cellar where it will be out of the weather, because there is a lot of good dressing there right now. I ought to note down on the calendar in my room that I saw the ewe named Galbreath go to buck day before yesterday, so I can have her lambing date. Hers will be the first lamb next spring, and it will be twins because she is a twinner. Which reminds me I ought to write Mike Galbreath a letter. I have been owing him one since before Roosevelt was elected for the third term. I certainly should do that, it has been such a long time. I should do it today while it is in my mind.

One thing I ought to do today is to take a small Stillson wrench and go down cellar and tighten the packing nut on the water pump so it won't drip. I could do that when I am down there making a place for the slabwood – it would save steps to combine the two things. I also ought to stir the litter in the henpen in the barn where the Barred Rocks are, and in the henhouse where the crossbred birds are; and then fill some bushel baskets with shavings and add them to the litter in the places where it needs deepening. The dropping boards under the broody coops need cleaning and I should do that at the same time, since I will be out there anyway. As far as litter is concerned, a man could take and rake the lawn under the maples where there is such an accumulation of leaves and add these dry leaves to the litter in the houses for the birds to scratch around in. Anything to keep their minds occupied in healthy channels.

Today I intend to pull the young alders in the field on the north side, as they are beginning to get ahead of me. I must do that today, probably later on this afternoon. A bush hook would be a good tool for that. I should also clean up the remaining garden trash and add it to the compost, saving out whatever the sheep might eat, and should remove the pipe from the well under the apple tree and store it down below in the barn.

I also think I had better call up a buyer and get rid of my ten old hens, since we have canned all we are going to need. After the hens are gone I shall no longer need the borrowed range house that they are living in, and I can get two long poles, lash them on behind the truck, and load the house on and drag it up to Kenneth's house. But it will be necessary to take an ax and flatten the ends of the poles so they won't dig into the highway, although the tar is so cold now they probably wouldn't dig in much anyway. Still, the thing to do is do it right.

Another thing I should try to manage to do today is to earmark the two pure-bred lambs. That will be easy enough – it just means finding the ear tags that I put away in a drawer or some place last spring and finding the special pliers that you have to use in squeezing a tag into a sheep's ear. I think I know where those pliers are, I think they are right in my cabinet next to that jar of rubber cement. I shall have to get the lambs up, but they will come without much trouble now because they are hungry. I *could* take the buck away at the same time if I could think of a place to put him.

Today I want to get word to Walter about the plowing of the garden pieces, and I had also better arrange down cellar about a bin for the roots, because on account of the extra amount of potatoes we have it will mean a little rearranging down there in order to get everything in. But I can do that when I am down tightening the nut on the pump. I ought to take the car into the village today to get an inspection sticker put on it; however, on second thought if I am going to the mill I guess it would be better to go in the truck and have a sticker put on *that* while I am seeing about the lumber, and then I can bring the boards back with me. But I mustn't be away at low water, otherwise I won't be able to hook on to the mooring.

Tomorrow is Tuesday and the egg truck will be coming through in the morning to pick up my cases, so I must finish grading and packing the eggs today – I have about fifty dozen packed and only ten to go to make up the two cases. Then I must nail up the cases and make out the tags and tack them on and lug the cases over to the cellar door, ready to be taken out in the morning, as the expressman is apt to get here early. I've also got to write a letter today to a publisher who wrote me asking what happened to the book manuscript I was supposed to turn in a year ago last spring, and I also should take the green chair in the living room to Eliot Sweet so that he can put in some little buttons that keep coming out all the time. I can throw the chair into the truck and drop it by his shop on my way to town. If I am going to take the squashes and pumpkins up to the attic I had better take the old blankets that we have been covering them with nights and hang them on the line to dry. I also ought to nail a pole up somewhere in the barn to hang grain sacks on so the rats won't be able to get at them and gnaw holes in them; empty sacks are worth ten cents for the heavy ones and five cents for the cotton ones, and they mount up quite fast and run into money. I mustn't forget to do that today – it won't take but a minute.

I've got to see about getting a birthday present for my wife today, but I can't think of anything. Her birthday is past anyway. There were things going on here at the time and I didn't get around to getting her a present but I haven't forgotten about it. Possibly when I am in the village I can find something.

If I'm going to rebuild the racks for the sheep it would be a good idea to have the mill rip out a lot of two-inch slats for me while I am there, as I shall need some stuff like that. I ought to make a list, I guess. And I mustn't forget shingle nails and the spikes. There is a place on the bottom step of the stairs going down into the woodshed where the crocus sack that I nailed on to the step as a foot-wiper is torn off, and somebody might catch his foot in that and take a fall. I certainly should fix that today before someone has a nasty fall. The best thing would be to rip the old sack off and tack a new one on. A man should have some roofing nails if he is going to make a neat job of tacking a sack on to a step. I think I may have some but I'd better look. I can look when I go out to get the Stillson wrench that I shall need when I go down to tighten the packing nut on the pump, and if I haven't any I can get some when I go to town.

I've been spending a lot of time here typing, and I see it is four o'clock already and almost dark, so I had better get going. Specially since I ought to get a haircut while I am at it. ❧

Forthcoming Topics

No. 3 ✦ Play
March, 2011

No. 4 ✦ Quiet
June, 2011

No. 5 ✦ Autumn
September, 2011

The Pedestrian welcomes the submission of essays to be considered for publication. The journal also welcomes editorial correspondence. For more information visit:

ThePedestrian.org/participate

Contributors

CHRIS ARTHUR is the author of *Irish Nocturnes*, *Irish Willow*, and *Irish Haiku*. Widely published as a poet and essayist on both sides of the Atlantic, his work has appeared in a range of literary journals including *The American Scholar*, *Descant*, *Irish Pages*, *The Literary Review*, *North American Review*, *Orion*, and the *Threepenny Review*. His work has been listed in the "Notable Essays" section of *Best American Essays* five times, and awarded the Akegarasu Haya International Essay Prize and Theodore Christian Hoepfner Award.

JOSEPH HILAIRE PIERRE BELLOC (1870-1953) was a prolific French-English writer of poetry and prose. His essay collections include *Hills and the Sea* (1906), *On Nothing & Kindred Subjects* (1908), *On Everything* (1909), *On Something* (1910), and *First and Last* (1911).

JENN BRISENDINE taught English literature and writing in a high school classroom for twelve years. She currently freelances and pursues fiction and non-fiction projects. Her essays appear in *Literary Mama*, the Seal Press anthology *The Maternal Is Political*, and *Mom Writer's Literary Magazine*. She lives in southwestern Pennsylvania with her husband, two sons, and a petite 100-pound Great Dane.

STEVEN CHURCH is the author of *The Day After The Day After: My Atomic Angst* (Soft Skull, 2010), *Theoretical Killings: Essays and Accidents*, and *The Guinness Book of Me*. His essays have been widely published, including recently in *Sonora Review*, *Brevity*, AGNI, *Fourth Genre*, and *Wag's Revue*. He's a founding editor of the literary magazine, *The Normal School*, and teaches in the MFA Program at Fresno State. He's currently working on a very long essay about ears.

JONATHAN FRANZEN is the author of four novels – *Freedom*, *The Corrections*, *The Twenty-Seventh City*, and *Strong Motion* – and two works of nonfiction, *How to Be Alone* and *The Discomfort Zone*, all published by Farrar, Straus and Giroux. He lives in New York City and Santa Cruz, California.

IAN FRAZIER is the author of *Travels in Siberia*, *Great Plains*, *The Fish's Eye*, *On the Rez*, and *Family*, as well as *Coyote v. Acme* and *Lamentations of the Father*. A frequent contributor to *The New Yorker*, he lives in Montclair, New Jersey.

DAVID MAMET was awarded the Pulitzer prize for his play *Glengarry Glen Ross*. His other plays and screenplays include *American Buffalo*, *The Untouchables*, *The Spanish Prisoner*, *Wag the Dog*, and *The Verdict*, the last two of which won Academy Award nominations. He has written a collection of poems, numerous essay collections, three novels, and a book of children's plays. He also created, produced, and wrote episodes of the television series *The Unit*.

CHRISTOPHER MORLEY (1890-1957) was an American journalist, novelist, essayist, and poet. His works include the essay collection *Pipefuls* (1920) and the novel *Kitty Foyle* (1939). Morley also assisted in revising the 11th and 12th editions of *Bartlett's Familiar Quotations*.

PHYLLIS ROSE is a biographer, essayist, literary critic, and portrait photographer. Her essays and literary criticism pieces have been published by *The New York Times*, *The Yale Review*, and *The American Scholar* among other publications. Rose was professor of English at Wesleyan University for more than 35 years. She currently photographs writers and artists.

SCOTT RUSSELL SANDERS is the author of twenty books of fiction and nonfiction, including, most recently, *A Private History of Awe*, which was nominated for the Pulitzer Prize, and *A Conservationist Manifesto*. Among his honors are the Lannan Literary Award, the John Burroughs Essay Award, the Mark Twain Award, and fellowships from the Guggenheim Foundation and the National Endowment for the Arts. He is a Distinguished Professor of English Emeritus at Indiana University, where he taught from 1971 to 2009.

LINDA SCHNEIDER is a professional calligrapher and watercolor artist working out of her studio in Liberty Lake, Washington. Ornate Pictorial Calligraphy, done with the pointed pen, is one of her favorite styles. She has been President of the *Scripts and Scribes Calligraphy Guild*, and is a member of the *International Association of Master Penmen, Engrossers, and Teachers of Handwriting*, where she has been part of the teaching faculty. She has authored the instructional book *Designing Faces, Figures, Florals and More*.

E.B. WHITE (1899-1985) is well known for two books popular with young readers: *Charlotte's Web* and *Stuart Little*. He also expanded and modernized William Strunk, Jr.'s *The Elements of Style*. Before these iconic works, his contributions to *Harper's* and *The New Yorker* were widely enjoyed. Of his clean and elegant writing White's friend, James Thurber, remarked, "No one can write a sentence like White."

ANDREW WILLSON was born and raised on the east side of Cleveland, Ohio and earned his BA at Case Western Reserve University. He has recently moved to New Haven, Connecticut where he is working on his PHD in English at Yale University. His essay in this issue, which was chosen as winner of The Pedestrian's Quarterly Essay Contest, is his first publication.

LIN YUTANG (1895-1976) is best known for his translations of Chinese classics into English for Western readers. A writer himself, he penned *The Importance of Living* and *Moment in Peking*. He created a new system for the romanization of the Chinese language and also created the first Chinese language typewriter, an accomplishment that took over a decade.

ZHUANGZI (c.369–c.286 BCE) is traditionally credited with having written the important and popular Taoist text that bears his name: the *Zhuangzi*.

Acknowledgments

Grateful acknowledgment is made for permission to reproduce the following copyrighted material:

Chris Arthur, "An Essay on the Essay" from *Irish Elegies* (Palgrave Macmillan, 2009). Copyright ©2009 by Chris Arthur. Reproduced by permission of Palgrave Macmillan.

Jonathan Franzen, "Scavenging" from *How to be Alone: essays* (Picador, 2003), modified from "Scavenging" in *The Antioch Review* (1996). Copyright © 2002, 2003 by Jonathan Franzen. Reproduced by permission of Farrar, Straus and Giroux.

Ian Frazier, "Bags in Trees", "Bags in Trees II", and "Bags in Trees: a retrospective" from *Gone to New York: adventures in the city* (Farrar, Straus and Giroux, 2005). Copyright ©2005 by Ian Frazier. Reproduced by permission of Farrar, Straus and Giroux.

David Mamet, "Knives" from *Jafsie and John Henry: essays* (Free Press, 1999). Copyright ©1999 by David Mamet. Reprinted by permission of the writer.

Phyllis Rose, "Tools of Torture" from *Never Say Goodbye* (Doubleday, 1991). Originally in The Atlantic (1987). Copyright ©1987, 1991 by Phyllis Rose. Reproduced by permission of the writer.

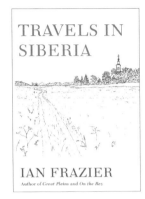

Irish Elegies

By CHRIS ARTHUR

June 2009 • 196 pages

ISBN: 978-0-230-61534-2

Hardcover Edition: $80.00

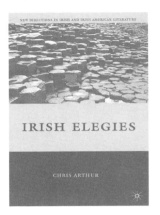

In this book, critically acclaimed author Chris Arthur continues his experiments with the mercurial literary genre of the essay, using it in innovative ways to explore aspects of family, place, memory, loss, and meaning. Through these unique prose meditations, readers are led to a dozen unexpected windows on Ireland.

"Arthur is a master essayist, adept at bringing his whole brain to bear on meaning-making.... As I came to the end of the book, I felt as if I had been sitting at the feet of a master, learning the ways of observation and meditation, as if I had been endowed with a new power for seeing beauty in everything around me, infused with the spirit of the essay."

—Patrick Madden, *Ploughshares*

ep;phany
a literary journal

S<small>HE HAD AN</small>
EPIPHANY.

H<small>OW ABOUT YOU</small>?

Subscribe at epiphanyzine.com

Or make a check payable to
Epiphany Magazine
and mail to:
71 Bedford St.

© Megan Pinch

Name _____

Address _____ Apt No. _____

City _____ State _____ Zip _____

Email _____

❑ One year $18   ❑ Two years $34   ❑ Three years $50

This issue's text is set in ADOBE JENSON PRO (1995), designed
by Robert Slimbach based upon Nicolas Jenson's roman,
cut in 1469, and Ludovico degli Arrighi's 1524 italic.
Footnotes are set in MYRIAD PRO (1992), designed
by Robert Slimbach & Carol Twombly.
The cover's text is set in CENTAUR MT
(2003), designed by Bruce Rogers
in 1914 and also modeled on
Jenson's roman face.

Artwork for the issue was contributed by
Linda Schneider.
www.LindaSchneiderArt.com

Letterpress printing of the cover by
Star Engraving & Printing Company
Houston, TX
www.starengraving.com

Offset printing of text and binding by
Branch-Smith Printing
Fort Worth, TX
www.branchsmithprinting.com